Tom Hutchinson

new hotline

intermediate

student's book

Key to symbols

▶1.2　Look at this part of the Grammar reference section, on pages 114-122.

Ω　This is a learning to learn activity.

Oxford University Press 1998

Contents

Unit theme / Learning preview	Victoria Road / Language work	Listening	Interaction	Reading	Guided writing	Pronunciation
Introduction 3–6	Structure revision	Andrea's first day				Phonetic alphabet: revision
1 Who are you? 7–16 Dealing with unknown words	Present tenses revision	Your secret personality Adverbs of frequency	Question forms: revision	The Greatest The past simple tense: revision	Paragraphs	-ty or -teen?
2 Travellers 17–26 Using a dictionary: 1	The present perfect tense Present perfect and past simple The present perfect continuous	Jenny's trip The past continuous tense	Talking about a trip Past and perfect tenses: questions	The Race to the Pole The past perfect tense	Sentence linking; personal letters	Reduced vowels
3 Ambitions 27–36 Using a dictionary: 2	Expressing the future	Work Reduced relative clauses	Gerunds: revision	So you want to be a pop star 'if' clauses (1)	Form and meaning	Syllable stress
4 Revision and project 37–40						Vowel revision
5 Motor mania 41–50 Parts of speech	The passive voice: revision 'used to'	The most unpopular men in London Modal verbs + passive	A parking incident	Auto-crazy Tenses in the passive voice	Topic sentences	Silent letters
6 Faraway places 51–60 Learning a foreign language	Question tags want someone to…	Journey to the stars Large numbers 'if' clauses (2)	Stranded	Oz Percentages and fractions	Showing contrast: 'but', 'however', 'although'	Intonation of question tags
7 Conflict 61–70 Group work	Reported speech: statements Reported speech: questions	Superheroes, super profits	Agreeing and disagreeing	The Cheetah's Eyes Indirect commands and requests	Reference	Word linking
8 Revision and project 71–74						Phonetic alphabet: revision
9 Image 75–84 Speaking English	There's sb …ing see/hear sb …ing	Image and colour	At the hairdresser's 'like'/'want' + present participle	Crowning glory 'by' + present participle	Summarising	Sentence stress
10 Mistakes 85–94 Coping with exams	'should/shouldn't have' 'should/shouldn't have been …ing' 'if' clauses (3)	Macbeth have something done	Responses	Oops! 'make'/'get'/'let'	Linking paragraphs	Silent /h/
11 Fame and fortune 95–104 How do you learn best?	Direct and indirect objects Passive with an indirect subject	Quiz show time 'one/ones'	Your quiz show	Champions	Formal letters	Strong and weak form prepositions
12 Revision 105–107						Phonetic alphabet: revision

Dictionary page 108–109   Pronunciation 110–113   Grammar reference 114–122   Wordlist 123–127

INTRODUCTION

Explore New Hotline

1 Look through the book. On which pages will you find these things?

- The Contents map
- Pronunciation practice activities
- The Grammar reference section
- The Dictionary page
- The Wordlist
- A list of irregular verbs

Learning preview

2 When you learn a language, your teacher and your textbook can help you, but if you want to learn a language well, you must also help yourself.

a What ways of helping yourself to learn do you already know?

b At the beginning of each unit you will find a 'Learning preview' task. Look at the Contents map and the unit openers. What aspects of learning will you learn about?

c At the end of each unit, you will find a Learning diary. Look at page 16.

- What does the Learning diary contain?
- What information would you put in your own Learning diary?

Victoria Road

3 Look at the picture.

a Who are the people? Look through the book and find their names.

b One of the characters isn't from Britain.
- Who is it?
- Where is he/she from? Look at the story on pages 4 and 5 and find out.

Andrea arrives

1 Read the introduction and look at the picture story.

a Who are the people?
b Where are they in each picture?
c What is happening?

Introduction

Sue and Vince Scott are at the airport. Sue has a Spanish penfriend called Carmen, and Carmen's cousin, who is from Argentina, is coming to stay with Sue and Vince's family. Sue and Vince are in the arrivals hall.

> What does this girl look like?

> I've got a photograph here. And she isn't 'this girl', Vince. Her name's Andrea.

1

2 Look at these lists. Read the full dialogue quickly. Match the names to the correct places.

Sue	Italy
Carmen	a sports shop
Terry	The Hartfield Academy
Vince	Oxford University
Andrea	Spain

3 🎧 Listen and follow in your book.

At the airport

Vince What does this girl look like?

Sue I've got a photograph here. And she isn't 'this girl', Vince. Her name's Andrea.

Vince Is that her over there now?

Sue Oh yes, it is. Andrea! Welcome to England.

Andrea Sue. I'm very pleased to meet you. And you must be Vince.

Vince That's right. Hi.

Sue Did you have a good flight, Andrea?

Andrea Yes. It was fine, thank you.

Vince Here. Let me help you with your luggage.

Sue Good idea, Vince. If you take the trolley, I'll fetch the car. I'll see you outside in a few minutes.

Outside

Vince What are you going to do here, Andrea? Sue told me, but I'm afraid I've forgotten.

Andrea I'm going to study English at a language school. It's called The Hartfield Academy.

Vince Your English is very good now. Have you been to Britain before?

Andrea No, I haven't, but Carmen tell … er I mean, has told me all about her visit, when Sue had had an accident, so there was nobody at the airport to meet her. And then she met um … oh, who's the boy who lives next door to you?

Vince Terry. Well, he isn't living next door at the moment.

> Andrea! Welcome to England.

> Sue. I'm very pleased to meet you.

2

Andrea Oh, is he still travelling round the world?

Vince I think so, but he doesn't write very often. We had a postcard from him a few weeks ago. He was visiting Italy then. He said they were on their way back to England, but he didn't say when he would arrive. I wouldn't be surprised if he turned up any day now.

Andrea Mm. Is Sue at Oxford University now?

Vince Yes. She's just home for the weekend.

Andrea And what about you, Vince? Aren't you going to university?

Vince Yes, I've been accepted by Nottingham, but I didn't want to go straight from school to university, so I decided to take a year out – you know – do something different.

VICTORIA ROAD

Andrea Oh, I see. So what do you do?

Vince Well, during the day I work in a shop that sells sports stuff – you know, trainers, tennis racquets and things like that. But that's just to earn some money. In the evenings I play the guitar with a band. We're practising one evening next week. You'll have to come along.

Andrea Mmm. That would be nice. I'd like that.

Later

Sue Well, here we are, Andrea, your home for the next year – number 18 Victoria Road.

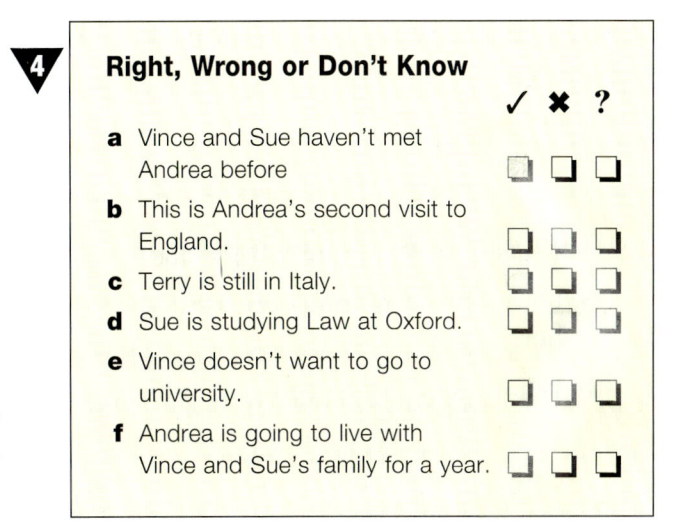

4

Right, Wrong or Don't Know   ✓ ✗ ?

a Vince and Sue haven't met Andrea before

b This is Andrea's second visit to England.

c Terry is still in Italy.

d Sue is studying Law at Oxford.

e Vince doesn't want to go to university.

f Andrea is going to live with Vince and Sue's family for a year.

What are you going to do here, Andrea? Sue told me, but I'm afraid I've forgotten.

I'm going to study English at a language school. It's called The Hartfield Academy.

Well, here we are, Andrea, your home for the next year – number 18 Victoria Road.

Useful expressions

5 How do you say these expressions in your language? Do you know any other English expressions with a similar meaning?

You must be ...

Let me help you (with ...)

I think so.

any day now

to take a year out

Oh, I see.

— optional activities —

6 a 📼 Close your book. Listen again.

b Work in groups of three. Each person takes one of the parts. Read the dialogue.

FOLLOW UP

7 Sue is writing to her friend, Kamala, who's gone to work in Canada. Copy and complete the letter.

...Well, that's enough about Oxford. Here's the news from Victoria Road. Carmen's .... Andrea arrived yesterday. She's from .... Vince .... I met her at the .... She's .... to study at a .... school called The Hartfield .... She .... living with us.

Terry's on .... way .... to England. We .... a postcard from him when he .... visiting Italy. He should be back .... day .... Casey's .... a teacher training college .... Manchester. Vince has .... accepted by Nottingham University, but he's .... a year out first. He's got a job in a .... shop and he .... the guitar .... a band.

How .... things with you in Canada?

LANGUAGE WORK

Structure revision

1 Do you recognize the tenses you have learnt?

a Look at this list of tenses.

present continuous present simple
present continuous past simple
past continuous present perfect
past perfect conditional

b Look through the Victoria Road story on pages 4 and 5. Find one example of each tense.

c Look through the story again. Find three ways of expressing the future.

d Find these things in the story.

two questions
two negative verbs
an **if** clause
an example of reported speech
an example of the passive
the future of 'must'
a relative clause

You will revise all of these structures and the different tenses in more detail through the book.

▶ Pronunciation: page 110

LISTENING

Andrea's first day

1 Look at the pictures.

a Where is Andrea? What is she doing?

b Listen to part 1 of the tape. Check your ideas.

c What do you think Andrea will say to the receptionist?

2 Listen to part 2 of the tape.

a What does Andrea say to the receptionist?

b What must she do?

c Listen to part 3 of the tape. Check your ideas.

— optional activity —

3 Listen to the whole tape again.

a Find two ways in which Andrea helps herself.

b What other things could she do?

4 Mr Robson asked Andrea a lot of questions. Use these cues to make the questions.

Example
Have you filled in the form?

fill in the form   any brothers or sisters
good journey   your parents/speak English
how long/flight   you/learn English at school
Britain/before   How old
your parents/do   do in England

— optional activity —

FOLLOW UP

5 Make your own conversation with Mr Robson. Use the cues in Exercise 4.

Learning objectives

Learning preview: Dealing with unknown words

Victoria Road: Talking about work and hobbies

Language work: The present simple and present continuous tenses ▶ 1.1 – 3

Listening: Describing personality
Adverbs of frequency ▶ 1.4

Interaction: Meeting someone and making conversation
Question forms

Reading: A biography
The past simple tense ▶ 1.5 – 7

Guided writing: Paragraph topics
Writing a biography

who are you?

1

Learning preview: *Dealing with unknown words*

1. Read this letter to the English learners' Problem Page.

   Dear Problem Page

   I want to learn English but I've got a big problem. Our teacher tells us that we should read as much as possible, but I can't read very fast. There are always words that I don't know, so I have to stop and look them up in my dictionary. It takes such a long time and it's very boring. What can I do?

   a What advice would you give the writer?

   b Report your ideas to the class. Make a class list of useful strategies for dealing with the problem.

Dealing with unknown words

2. Try to follow the advice yourself as you work through the unit.

Kim

1 Look at the picture story.

  a Where does this episode take place?

  b What are the people doing there?

  c What are the names of the three new characters?

  d What does each person do in the group?

2 Put these sentences in the correct order to match the story.

  A Kim arrives.
  B Andrea stands in for Kim.
  C Vince and Andrea go to the church hall.
  D Kim takes the microphone from Andrea.
  E Andrea meets Dan and Rosy.
  F Vince introduces Andrea to Kim.

3 Listen and follow in your book.

Vince We practise in a church hall near Dan's place. Dan's our drummer. I usually take the car, but Dad's mending it – again! So we'll have to take the bus, I'm afraid. Fortunately all the gear's already there.

At the church hall

Vince Andrea, this is Dan.

Dan Hi, Andrea.

Andrea Hello.

Vince And this is Rosy. She plays the keyboards.

Rosy Hi. Nice to meet you, Andrea.

Andrea You play the guitar, don't you, Vince?

Vince Yes, I play the bass guitar. Hey, where's Kim?

Dan Surprise, surprise. She isn't here yet. She's always late.

Vince Well, I imagine she's working late tonight.

Rosy Kim's Vince's girlfriend.

Andrea Oh, I see. What does she do?

Rosy She sings. She's got a good voice.

Andrea No, I meant, what's her job?

Rosy Oh, I see. Sorry. She works in a hairdresser's in the High Street. Dan doesn't like her very much. But I think she's OK. I mean, nobody's perfect.

Vince OK. Well, let's get started.

Dan But we can't do much without a singer.

Vince You can sing, can't you, Andrea? When I was practising the other night, you sang some of the numbers for me.

Andrea Well, yes, I know some songs, but …

Vince Would you mind standing in for Kim till she gets here? Here's the first number and there's the mike. Thanks.

Rosy All right. From the top.

1. We practise in a church hall near Dan's place. Dan's our drummer. I usually take the car, but Dad's mending it – again! So we'll have to take the bus, I'm afraid. Fortunately all the gear's already there.

2. And this is Rosy. She plays the keyboards.
   Hi. Nice to meet you, Andrea.

VICTORIA ROAD

Andrea There he was just a-walking down the street, singing, 'Do wah diddy …'

After the song

Rosy Hey, you're pretty good, Andrea.

Dan I don't like it, Vince. Oh, I don't mean your singing, Andrea. That was great. But we really need a rhythm or lead guitar. It doesn't sound rich enough.

Vince Ah, here's Kim.

Kim Hi, guys. Sorry I'm late. Oh, I see you've already got a new singer. I didn't realize I was that late.

Vince Kim, this is Andrea. She was just standing in for you. Andrea's my sister's penfriend's cousin. She's from Argentina.

Andrea Hello, Kim. Pleased to meet you.

Kim Hi. Are you on holiday?

Andrea No, I'm studying English at The Hartfield Academy.

Kim Oh yes, I know it. Where are you staying?

Vince Andrea's living with us while she's here.

Kim Oh! How nice, Vince!

What do you think?

- Do you think Kim is often late? Why?
- What do you think about the relationships within the group?
- How does Kim feel about Andrea?

4 Complete the sentences with the correct subjects.

a .... is mending the car.

b .... take the bus.

c .... complains that Kim is late again.

d .... tells Andrea about Kim.

e .... stands in for Kim.

f .... thinks that the group needs another guitar.

g .... isn't very pleased about Andrea living with the Scotts.

Would you mind standing in for Kim till she gets here? Here's the first number and there's the mike. Thanks.

Hey, where's Kim?

Surprise, surprise. She isn't here yet.

Kim's Vince's girlfriend.

3

Hi, guys. Sorry I'm late. Oh, I see you've already got a new singer. I didn't realize I was that late.

Kim, this is Andrea. She was just standing in for you.

5

4

Andrea's living with us while she's here.

Oh! How nice, Vince!

6

Useful expressions

5 How do you say these expressions in your language? Do you know any other English expressions with a similar meaning?

Nobody's perfect.

Let's get started.

Would you mind ...ing?

From the top.

You're pretty good.

Sorry I'm late.

---- optional activities ----

LANGUAGE USE

6 Look at Kim's last line.

Oh! How nice, Vince!

Kim is being sarcastic. When we're being sarcastic we usually say the opposite of what we really mean.

a Does Kim really think it's nice?

b Find an example of where Dan is sarcastic. What does he really mean?

7 a 📼 Close your book. Listen again.

b Work in groups of four. One person is Vince, one person is Andrea, one person is Dan and one person is Rosy and Kim. Read the dialogue.

FOLLOW UP

8 Answer these questions.

a Where does the group usually practise?
b Why aren't Vince and Andrea going by car?
c What instrument does Rosy play?
d How does Dan feel about Kim?
e Where does Kim work?
f How does Vince know that Andrea can sing?
g Why doesn't Dan like the sound of the number?

LANGUAGE WORK

Present tenses: revision ▶ 1.1–3

1 What do you know about the present simple tense?

a Look at these sentences from the Victoria Road story on pages 8 and 9.

And this is Rosy. She plays the keyboards.
I play the bass guitar.

b Explain the difference. Give the rule for the **-s** ending in the present simple tense.

c Find more examples of the present simple tense in the story.

d Copy and complete these two sentences from the Victoria Road story.

Dan .... like her very much.
I .... like it, Vince.

e Explain the rule for making the present simple negative.

- When do we use **don't** and when do we use **doesn't**?
- What happens to the **-s** ending?

Example
Vince likes her.
Dan doesn't like her.

▶ 1.1 Check your rules in the Grammar reference section.

2 Rosy is talking to Andrea. Complete her statements with the verbs in brackets.

a We .... at local dances and things like that. (play)

b Kim .... on the other side of town. (live)

c Dan's a student. He .... to Hartfield Technical College. (go)

d I'm a student, too. I .... to London University. (go)

e I .... in the same shop as Vince on Saturdays. (work)

f Dan and Vince .... football together. (play)

g You .... very well. (sing)

3 Some of these sentences are incorrect. Put the verbs into the negative to make true sentences where necessary.

a Kim goes to London University.
b Vince and Rosy work in a hairdresser's.
c Dan lives in Victoria Road.
d Rosy likes Kim.
e They practise at Dan's house.
f Kim plays the guitar.
g Dan and Kim like each other.

4 What other present tense do you know?

a Look at these two sentences from the Victoria Road story. What are the two tenses?

She **works** in a hairdresser's in the High Street. She**'s working** late tonight.

b Why is the tense different in the two sentences? Explain the difference in meaning.

c Some verbs do not have a continuous form. Look at the Grammar reference (1.3) for examples of these verbs.

d Find examples of non-continuous verbs in the Victoria Road story.

e Note: Kim asks 'Where are you staying?' She uses the continuous tense to talk about a temporary state.

5 Complete these sentences. Put the verbs in brackets into the correct tense.

a Vince usually .... to practice sessions on his own, but tonight he .... Andrea with him. (go/take)

b He .... to take his dad's car, but his father .... it, so they .... on the bus. (want/mend/go)

c Kim .... late this evening. She normally .... work at six o'clock. (work/finish)

d The band usually .... the same songs, but tonight Dan .... they .... right. (play/not think/sound)

e Kim .... it when she .... that Andrea .... at Vince's house. (not like/realize/live)

6 Choose the correct tense of the verbs.

My favourite group are called Hard Times. They *come/are coming* from our town. In this picture they *play/are playing* at our school dance. My favourite member is Carl. He's the guy who *wears/is wearing* the green shirt. He *looks/is looking* really gorgeous here, I *think/am thinking*.

Hard Times are not a famous group. They only *play/are playing* at local dances and things like that, but my friends and I all *agree/are agreeing* that they're going to be big one day. We *go/are going* to all their gigs. We *think/are thinking* they *sound/are sounding* great. Today they *play/are playing* in the local park. We *go/are going* to see them.

— optional activity —

FOLLOW UP

7 Write about your favourite pop group.

a Give this information about them.

Where are they from?
What does each member of the group do?
Why do you like them?
Who is your favourite member of the group?

b Find a picture of the group. Write about the picture.

Where are they playing?
What are they wearing?

LISTENING

Your secret personality

1 Read this paragraph. What is it about?

Everyone has got two personalities – the one that they show to the world and their secret, real personality. You don't show your secret personality when you're awake because you can control your behaviour, but when you're asleep, your sleeping position shows the real you. In a normal night, of course, people frequently change their position. The important position is the one that you go to sleep in.

— optional activity —

2 Look at the four sleeping positions.

a Which position do you usually go to sleep in?

b Ask other members of your class:

'Which position do you go to sleep in?'

3 Look at the list of personality traits above the pictures.

a Use a dictionary. Find the meaning of any words or expressions that you don't know.

b 📼 Listen and match the personality traits to the correct position.

Adverbs of frequency ▶ 1.4

4 Look at these words. They say how often something happens.

always   usually   normally   often
sometimes   never

a Look at these sentences from the tape.

1 You express your real feelings.
2 You're easily upset.
3 You're defensive.
4 You don't like meeting people.
5 People who sleep on their side have got a well-balanced personality.
6 You feel anxious.

b 📼 Listen again. Where do the adverbs of frequency go in the sentences in **a**?

Example

never
You / express your real feelings.

c Where do we put the adverbs of frequency? Make a rule for their position.

- with the verb **to be**
- with an auxiliary verb (such as **have**, **don't**)
- with other verbs

— optional activity —

FOLLOW UP

5 Write the sentences in Exercise 4 with the adverbs of frequency in the correct position.

---

a You're very nervous.
b You're very open.
c You're secretive.
d You trust people.
e You're defensive.
f You're shy.
g You don't express your real feelings.
h You worry a lot.
i You feel anxious.
j You aren't very confident.
k You don't like meeting people.
l You're easily upset.
m You don't get depressed.
n You're very stubborn.
o You live for today.
p You're easily hurt.

1 on your back
2 on your stomach
3 curled up
4 on your side

INTERACTION

Question forms: revision

▶ 1.1–3

1 Look at the Victoria Road story on pages 8 and 9.

  a Find examples of questions with:
  - the verb to be
  - the present simple
  - the present continuous

  b Explain the rules for making these questions.

2 Complete the dialogue.

  a Use the cues to make questions.

  b Read the dialogue with a partner.

Sally Hi. I'm Sally. (What/name)?
Julio Julio. Pleased to meet you.
Sally (Where/from)?
Julio I'm from Portugal.
Sally (on holiday)?
Julio Yes, I am.
Sally (Who/stay with)?
Julio I'm staying with my penfriend, Mark.
Sally (Where/he/live)?
Julio In Minster Road. (know/it)?
Sally Yes, I do. (Mark/go/to West Street school)?
Julio Yes, that's right.
Sally (like/it here)?
Julio Yes, it's great.
Sally (do/anything/Saturday evening)?
Julio No, I don't think so.
Sally A friend of mine is having a party. (want/to come)?
Julio Sure. (What time/start)?
Sally I'll call you. (What/phone number)?
Julio It's 64921.

3 You are in another country. You meet a boy or girl. You want to get to know him/her. Make the conversation.

  a Make an imaginary character for yourself. You should decide:
  - your name
  - where you are from
  - who you are staying with

  b Work in pairs.
  - Introduce yourself.
  - Find out some information about the other person.
  - Find out some information about the people that the other person is staying with.
  - Arrange to meet the other person again.

  c Find another partner and repeat.

—— optional activities ——

FOLLOW UP

4 Write one of your dialogues from Exercise 3.

5 📼 Here's a song about meeting someone.

  a What do you think the missing words are?

  b Listen and check your ideas.

Do wah diddy diddy

There he .... just a-walking down the street.
Singing do wah diddy diddy dum diddy do.
Snapping his fingers and shuffling his ....
Singing do wah diddy diddy dum diddy do.
He looked ....
He looked ....
He .... good, he looked fine
And I nearly .... my mind.

Before I knew it he was walking next to ....
Singing do wah diddy diddy dum diddy do.
Holding my hand just as natural as could ....
Singing do wah diddy diddy dum diddy do.
We .... on
To my ....
We walked on to my door, then we ....
a little more.

Wo oh wo oh
I knew we were .... in love.
Wo wo wo wo Yes I ....
And so I told .... all the things
that I've been dreaming of.

Now we're together nearly every single ....
Singing do wah diddy diddy dum diddy do.
We're so .... and that's how we're gonna stay
Singing do wah diddy diddy dum diddy do.
Cos I'm ....
He's ....
I'm his and he's mine. Wedding .... are gonna chime.

READING

1 Look quickly at the text.

a Who is it about?

b What do you already know about him?

2 Read the text. What happened in each of these years? Write down as many things as possible.

1963   1969   1981   1984
1986   1991   1996

The Greatest

Michael Jordan grabbed the ball from his opponent's hands. He raced down the court and jumped. What did he do? Did he put the ball straight into the basket? Was it just another two points for the greatest basketball player in the world? No. Michael Jordan wanted to show why he was the greatest. In the air he turned. Then, with his back to the basket, he took the ball in both hands and threw it backwards over his head. SLAM! The ball was in the basket.

Michael Jordan was born in New York in February 1963, but he grew up in Wilmington, North Carolina. He wasn't a brilliant student at school. 'I sometimes got into trouble,' he says, 'because I didn't do my schoolwork.' But he loved sports. He first played basketball in the family's back garden. When Michael was six years old, his father built two basketball goals, and Michael played there with his brothers and his friends.

He played basketball at school, and when he went to the University of North Carolina in 1981 he joined the basketball team. By this time he was 1.98 metres tall. In 1984 he won a gold medal as a member of the United States Olympic basketball team. A few weeks later he left university and became a professional player with the Chicago Bulls. But he didn't forget his education. He returned to the university for two summers and finished his degree in 1986.

As a professional Michael Jordan amazed the crowds with his skill. He earned millions of dollars on the basketball court, and he made millions more from advertising trainers, drinks, cars and many other things. In 1991 the Bulls were the National Basketball Association champions. In 1996 Michael starred in the film 'Space Jam'.

Although he is an international star, Michael Jordan leads a simple life. He lives in Chicago with his wife, Juanita, and their three children. He likes to play golf and to cook. He also does a lot to help children from poor homes. He tells them: 'Stay away from drugs and alcohol and get the best education you can.'

3 Read the text again. Find all the information about these things.

- Michael's education
- his family
- his achievements

— optional activity —

WORD WORK

4 Look through the text.

a Find all the words in the text associated with sport.

b Add six more words associated with your favourite sport to the list.

The past simple tense: revision ▶ 1.5–7

5 A lot of the verbs in the text are in the past simple tense.

a Find examples of these things.

For the verb 'to be':
- a positive statement
- a negative statement
- a question

For other verbs:
- a regular verb
- an irregular verb
- a negative statement
- a question

b Use your examples. Explain the rules for making each one.

c Complete these sentences. Put the verbs in brackets into the past simple tense.

1 Michael .... still a baby when the family .... to Wilmington. (be/move)

2 He .... school very much and he often .... into trouble. (not like/get)

3 People .... amazed when they first .... Michael Jordan. (be/see)

4 He .... jump higher than anyone else. (can)

5 He .... the ball from his opponent's hands and .... it. (knock/grab)

6 In 1985 he .... a bone in his foot and he .... for most of the season. (break/not play)

7 He .... Juanita in 1989. (marry)

6 Here is part of an interview with Michael Jordan.

a Complete the questions to match the answers.

Interviewer When .... ?

Michael Jordan In 1963.

Interviewer Where .... ?

Michael Jordan I grew up in Wilmington, North Carolina.

Interviewer .... ?

Michael Jordan No, I wasn't. I often missed lessons.

Interviewer Where .... ?

Michael Jordan In our back garden. My dad built two basketball goals there.

Interviewer ....

Michael Jordan Yes, I went to the University of North Carolina.

b Add four more questions and answers.

c Role play the interview.

— optional activity —

FOLLOW UP

7 What do you think are the most interesting things about Michael Jordan and his life story? Write ten sentences about him.

GUIDED WRITING

Paragraphs

1 Look at the text on page 14.

a How many paragraphs has it got?

b What is the topic of each paragraph? Put these topics in the correct order.

- A his lifestyle
- B his amateur career
- C an incident during a game
- D his early life
- E his professional career

c Here is some more information about Michael Jordan. In which paragraph would you put each one? Why?

1 In the 1986–7 season he scored more than 3,000 points. Only one other player had ever done that before.
2 He particularly likes French and Italian food.
3 He passed the ball from hand to hand.
4 The crowd cheered and shouted: 'Michael! Michael! Michael!'.
5 In 1983 *Sporting News* named him College Player of the Year.
6 He was the third of four children.
7 People who never watched basketball knew his face from TV adverts.

2 Look at the order of the paragraphs.

a Why are paragraphs 2–5 in this order? Look at the dates and the verb tenses.

b Now look at paragraph 1. This doesn't follow the same order. Why do you think it comes first?

A biography of a star

3 Write a biography of another famous sports, pop or film star. It can be a real or an imaginary person. Use the paragraph structure above.

— optional activity —

Project suggestion

4 Illustrate your biography with some pictures of your star. Invent an interview with him/her and put it with your biography.

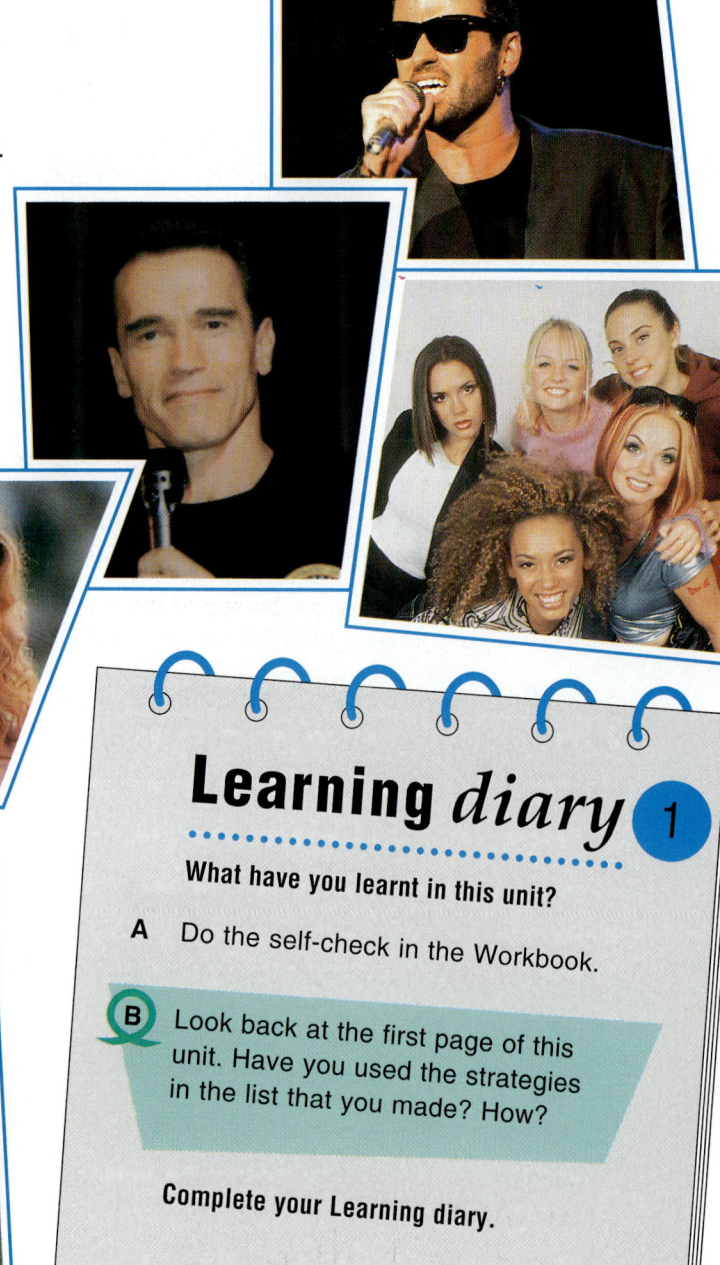

Learning *diary* 1

What have you learnt in this unit?

A Do the self-check in the Workbook.

B Look back at the first page of this unit. Have you used the strategies in the list that you made? How?

Complete your Learning diary.

▶ Pronunciation: page 110

2 travellers

Learning objectives

Learning preview: Using a dictionary: 1

Victoria Road: Catching up on news

Language work: The present perfect and past simple tenses ▶ 2.1–3
The present perfect continuous tense ▶ 2.4

Listening: Describing a trip
The past continuous tense ▶ 2.5–6

Interaction: Talking about a trip

Reading: A story of exploration
The past perfect tense ▶ 2.7–8

Guided writing: Sentence linking
Personal letters

Learning preview: *Using a dictionary: 1*

A dictionary is a useful learning tool if you use it properly. First you need to find your word.

1 Look at the dictionary extract on pages 108–9. Answer these questions.

   a What are the words at the top of the page?
   b Why are they there?

2 Close the dictionary page and do these tasks.

   a Will you find these words in the extract?

   fire   first   get   fine   fall   film   finger

   b Put these words in the order that they will come in the dictionary.

   fir   find   finish   fire   fiord   finely

   c Under which entry in the dictionary will you find these?

   have something at your fingertips   finely
   She finished with her boyfriend.   firewood
   an oil-fired power station

   d The meaning of **snap your fingers** is not given. Where will you find it?

3 There are two entries for 'find out'.

   a What are the two entries?
   b What do you think **sb** and **sth** mean?

The rover returns

1 Look at the picture story.

  a Who is in this episode?

  b Where are they?

2 Match the subjects to the correct sentence endings.

Mr Scott	has been on a trip round the world.
Terry	needs another guitarist.
Shirley	thinks Terry causes problems.
The band	invites Terry to a practice session.
Rosy	saw Terry last night.
Vince	taught Terry to play the guitar.

3 Listen and follow in your book.

Vince Well, well, well, look who it is. Great to see you, Terry. When did you get back?

Terry Last night. I saw your dad outside. He was mending the car. He said you were out.

Vince Yes, that's right.

Terry Has he been mending that car all the time I've been away? He was doing it the day I left, too.

Vince It sometimes seems like it.

Rosy Ahem!

Vince Oh, sorry! Terry, this is Rosy.

Rosy Hello, Terry. You've been on a trip round the world or something, haven't you?

Terry Yes, that's right.

Rosy How long have you been away?

Terry Just under a year.

Rosy Where did you go?

Terry Oh, loads of places. We went to South America, round Cape Horn. Then on to New Zealand and Australia and …

Rosy That sounds wonderful! Victoria Road must seem a bit dull after that, I suppose.

Hello, Terry. You've been on a trip round the world or something, haven't you?

Yes, that's right.

Well, well, well, look who it is. Great to see you, Terry. When did you get back?

Last night. I saw your dad outside. He was mending the car. He said you were out.

Terry Well, yes. But we weren't visiting places all the time. We were on the ship most of the time, you see.

Rosy Didn't you get seasick?

Terry No! I've got an iron stomach. Anyway, there was a lot to do on the ship. And there were some really interesting people on board, I mean, one of the girls – Shirley her name was – taught me how to play the guitar.

Rosy Oh, that's lucky. We've got a band, you know, and we've been looking for an extra guitarist. Are you any good?

Terry Well, Shirley had played with a lot of sort of famous bands, before she went on the trip, and she said I wasn't bad.

VICTORIA ROAD

3 And there were some really interesting people on board, I mean, one of the girls – Shirley her name was – taught me how to play the guitar.

Oh, that's lucky. We've got a band, you know, and we've been looking for an extra guitarist.

4 Well ... look, we'd better be off, Rosy. I ...

Why don't you come to one of our practice sessions next week?

5 Anyway, Vince, what's been happening here, while I've been away?

Oh, I'll tell you all about that later, Terry. We've, er, got to go. We're on our lunch break, you see.

6 He's rather nice, your friend Terry. And I bet you're pleased that he can play the guitar.

Well, I'm not so sure. You don't know Terry like I do.

What do you mean?

Oh, things just have a habit of going wrong when Terry's around, somehow.

Vince Well ... look, we'd better be off, Rosy, I ...

Rosy Why don't you come to one of our practice sessions next week?

Terry Thanks, I will. Anyway, Vince, what's been happening here, while I've been away?

Vince Oh, I'll tell you all about that later, Terry. We've, er, got to go. We're on our lunch break, you see.

Outside

Rosy He's rather nice, your friend Terry. And I bet you're pleased that he can play the guitar.

Vince Well, I'm not so sure. You don't know Terry like I do.

Rosy What do you mean?

Vince Oh, things just have a habit of going wrong when Terry's around, somehow.

What do you think?

- What does Rosy think about Terry?
- How does Vince feel about Terry joining the group?

▼4 Answer these questions.

a Why didn't Vince see Terry last night?

b How long has Terry been away?

c What places did he visit?

d How well can Terry play the guitar?

e Why do Rosy and Vince have to leave?

f Why is Vince worried?

Useful expressions

5 How do you say these expressions in your language? Do you know any other English expressions with a similar meaning?

Look who it is.

loads of ...   It seems like it.

We'd better be off.   Are you any good?

like I do

---

optional activities

LANGUAGE USE

6 Conversations often have a lot of fillers, like 'Well' and 'I suppose'. They don't have any meaning, but they make the conversation smoother and less formal.

a Find some more fillers in the story.

b What fillers does your language have?

7 a 🔊 Close your book. Listen again.

b Work in groups of three. Each person takes one part. Read the dialogue.

FOLLOW UP

8 Complete Rosy's conversation with Kim.

Rosy I met Vince's .... Terry, today. He came .... the cafe while Vince and I were on our lunch ....

Kim What's he .... ?

Rosy I think he's .... nice. He's .... on a trip round .... world. He only .... back last night. He went to .... of wonderful places – South .... , Australia and New .... And guess what? He can play .... guitar. A girl that was .... board .... him.

LANGUAGE WORK

The present perfect tense

▶ 2.1

1 These sentences are in the present perfect.

You've been on a trip round the world.
You haven't met Rosy before.
How long have you been away?

a Rewrite the sentences with Terry as the subject. What changes?

b How do we form these things in the present perfect tense?
- positive statements
- negative statements
- questions

▶ 2.1 Check your rules in the Grammar reference section.

2 a Look at this list. Has Terry done these things in the past year? Have you done them?

Example
Terry has been on a trip round the world.
I haven't been on a trip round the world.

be on a trip round the world   travel on a ship
visit another country   learn Russian
make some/any new friends   be seasick
play a musical instrument

b Work with a partner. Ask and answer.

Example
Has Terry been on a trip round the world?
Yes, he has.
Have you been on a trip round the world?
No, I haven't.

Present perfect and past simple ▶ 2.2–3

3 Look at these pairs of sentences. Explain why the past simple or the present perfect is used in each case.

1 I've seen that film. I saw it last week.
2 He's broken his wrist. He fell off his bike.
3 We've had a lot of telephone calls today. Nobody called yesterday.

▶ 2.2–3 Check your rules in the Grammar reference section.

4 Vince is telling Terry about what has happened while he has been away. Work in pairs. Use these cues. Make their conversation.

Terry I/not see/Sue/yet

Vince Sue/go/to Oxford

Terry When/she/go?

Vince She/leave/last month

Terry Oh, I see. How long/you/have/a band?

Vince We/form/the band about six months ago. By the way, you/meet/Andrea yet?

Terry Yes, I/see/her this morning. How long/she/be/here?

Vince She/arrive/last Sunday, so she/be/here for about a week now

The present perfect continuous ▶ 2.4

5 The sentences below are from the Victoria Road story on pages 18 and 19.

a Copy and complete them.

A .... that car all the time I've been away?

B ....for an extra guitarist.

C What .... here, while I've been away?

We call this the present perfect continuous tense. We use the present perfect continuous tense to describe a long or continuous activity in the past that has continued up to the present.

b Copy and complete this table.

I You We They	have not 've	....	travelling round the world mending the car.
He She It	has .... hasn't		looking for a guitarist. having a good time.

c Look at the sentences in **a** above. How do we make questions in the present perfect continuous?

6 What have these people been doing?

1 2 3 4 5 6

a Work in pairs. Ask the people in the pictures what they have been doing.

Example
A *What have you been doing?*   B *I've been ...*

b One student thinks of an activity and says something about his/her present state. The other student must ask questions to find out what he/she has been doing.

Example
A *I feel tired and my feet hurt.*
B *Have you been jogging?*
A *No, I haven't.*
B *Have you been ... ?*

─ optional activity ─

FOLLOW UP

7 Answer the questions in full sentences.

a What have you been doing for the last hour?

b How long have you been learning English?

c What do you think your parents have been doing for the last hour?

d What do you think your favourite pop star has been doing today?

LISTENING

Jenny's trip

1 You are going to hear a conversation between Bill and Jenny.

a Look at these sentences.

Jenny has been to Germany.
She was working in a hotel there.
She had an accident while she was there.
She came home a month ago.

b 📼 Listen. Say whether the sentences are right or wrong.

2 Work with a partner. What can you remember?

a Write down everything that you can remember about the conversation.

b Compare your ideas with another pair.

c 📼 Listen again and check your ideas.

── optional activity ──

3 There are a lot of response expressions and fillers in the dialogue.

a Here are some of Bill's responses. Match them to Jenny's statements.

I've been away.
I've been to Germany.
About ten months.
I was studying German at the university.
I had an accident a couple of days after I arrived.
But it wasn't serious. Just a shock really, I suppose.
I went to loads of places and I went to Denmark and Poland, too.

Very nice!
That sounds interesting.
That was lucky.
Oh, I see.
That's a long time
Great!
Oh dear!

b Which of these fillers does Jenny use?

I think   you see   I suppose   you know
well   anyway   I mean   sort of

c 📼 Listen again and check your ideas.

The past continuous tense

▶ 2.5–6

4 Complete the sentences. Choose from these verbs:

was stepping   was crossing   ran   crossed
stepped   was running

A While I .... the street, a cyclist .... into me.

B I .... into the road and a cyclist .... into me.

a Look at your completed sentences. What tenses are used?

b Why are the tenses different in the first sentence but the same in the second?

c Look at these sentences. Why do you think the past continuous tense is used?

What were you doing there?
I was studying German.

▶ 2.5–6 Check your rules in the Grammar reference section.

5 Look at the cues. Say what other things happened to Jenny.

a walk in a forest in Poland/see a bear/take a photograph
b sit in a cafe/meet an old friend/have a long chat
c shop/lose her keys/someone/find them
d live in Germany/speak German all the time/learn a lot
e visit Denmark/car/break down/have to sleep in the car

── optional activity ──

FOLLOW UP

6 Bill is telling somebody about his conversation with Jenny. What does he say?

INTERACTION

Talking about a trip

1 Here are Bill's questions from his conversation with Jenny.

a Copy and complete them. Put the verbs in brackets into the correct tense.

b 🔊 Listen and check your ideas.

I've been away.
Where .... ? (be)
How long .... there for? (be)
.... in Berlin? (be)
What .... there? (do)
.... it? (enjoy)
What .... ? (happen)
.... any other places while you were out there? (visit)
How long .... back? (be)
What .... since you got back? (do)

Past and perfect tenses: questions ▶ 2.1–5

2 How do we make questions in these tenses?

- the past simple
- the past continuous
- the present perfect
- the present perfect continuous

a Work with a partner. Write rules for each tense. Use the questions in Exercise 1 to illustrate your rules.

b Compare your ideas with another pair's.

▶ 2.1–5 Check your rules in the Grammar reference section.

3 Look at the information about two other trips below.

	A	B
Country	Canada	France
How long?	six months	three months
Place	Vancouver	near Nice
Why?	study English at language school	work in a holiday village
Enjoy?	Yes/people very friendly	Yes/meet/a lot of interesting people
Incident	ski/meet neighbour/he/on holiday meet/have long chat	swim/someone steal wallet/report to police/not get back
Visit	lots of places in Canada and USA	Marseilles/Italy/Switzerland
Return	three weeks/just before Christmas	five weeks/in September
Since return	revise for exam	look for a job

a Work with a partner. You meet a friend that you haven't seen for a while. Use the questions in Exercise 1 and the information in column A. Make the dialogue. Start like this.

Hi, I haven't seen you for a long time.
Yes, well, I've been away.

b Reverse roles and repeat with the information in column B.

---- optional activity ----

FOLLOW UP

4 You have just come back from a trip and you are talking to a friend about it. Make the dialogue. Follow the pattern in Exercise 3.

READING

> **optional activity**
>
> **1 Discuss these questions.**
>
> a What famous explorers do you know? Which parts of the world did they explore?
>
> b The text below is about the first person to reach the South Pole. Do you know who it was?
>
> c If you were going to the South Pole, what plans would you make?
> - What form of transport would you use?
> - What would you need to take with you?
> - What problems might there be?

2 Read the text.

a Match the names of the explorers to the countries.

Scott	Norway
Amundsen	Italy
Peary	Britain
Nobile	the USA

b Who do you think the people in the pictures are? Why?

The Race to the Pole

1 It was October 1911 and in Antarctica Captain Robert Scott and eleven companions were setting off to the South Pole. Nobody had ever reached the Pole before. In front of them lay 1400 kilometres of snow and ice.

2 However, Scott had a rival – the Norwegian explorer, Roald Amundsen. Amundsen had originally planned an expedition to the North Pole, but the American explorer, Robert E. Peary, had beaten him to it. So Amundsen had changed his plans and sailed south to the Antarctic.

3 The two expeditions were very different. Scott had chosen horses to pull his group's sledges. He also had a few motor sledges. Food and fuel for the expedition had already been placed along the first part of the route. Amundsen, however, set off with only four companions and 52 dogs to pull their sledges. They didn't take a lot of food with them. When the men and the dogs needed food, they killed one of the dogs and ate it.

4 Scott's expedition started badly. The motor sledges broke down and the horses couldn't survive in the cold weather. Scott sent most of the team back to the base. Then he and four companions walked the rest of the journey pulling their own sledge.

5 .... reached the Pole first and when .... group finally arrived, they found a .... flag there. Bitterly disappointed, they started the journey back to the base, but they never reached it. Just 18 kilometres from the base they were trapped in their tent by a terrible snowstorm and died there.

6 As for .... , he returned home as a hero. Then in 1928 he learnt that his friend, Nobile, an Italian explorer had disappeared in the Arctic. .... set off by plane to look for him. Nobile was later found alive, but .... was never seen again.

3 Look at the last two paragraphs.

a Which of the explorers do you think:
- was the first person to reach the South Pole?
- died in the Antarctic?
- died in the Arctic?

b 🔊 Listen. Find the missing names.

4 Answer these questions.

a How far did Scott travel?
b Why did Amundsen change his plans?
c Why didn't Amundsen's team put food and fuel on the route?
d Why did Scott change his plans?
e How did the second group know that they had been beaten?
f How did Scott and Amundsen die?

The past perfect tense ▶ 2.7–8

5 Look at these sentences.

Nobody had ever reached the South Pole before.
Peary had beaten him to it.

a The verbs in these sentences are in the past perfect tense. How do we make the tense?

b The story starts in October 1911. Look at the first four paragraphs. Which tense is used to talk about:
- events in October 1911?
- events before October 1911?

c Why is each tense used?

▶ 2.7–8 Check your rules in the Grammar reference section.

6 Put the verbs in brackets into the past simple or the past perfect tense.

a Scott and Amundsen .... to go to the South Pole, because nobody .... it before. (want/reach)

b Amundsen .... much faster, because he .... to use dogs not ponies. (travel/decide)

c Not many of the dogs .... back, because the men .... them. (come/eat)

d Scott's men .... their own sledge, because Scott .... the rest of the party back to base. (pull/send)

e When Amundsen .... that his friend .... , he .... to find him. (learn/disappear/try)

f Scott .... to the Antarctic twice before 1911. (be)

g When Scott and his companions .... the Pole they .... 1400 kilometres. (reach/travel)

---

optional activities

WORD WORK

7 Find all the words in the text associated with:
- travel
- the Antarctic

FOLLOW UP

8 Copy and complete these sentences.

a .... decided to go to the Antarctic when ...
b .... walked most of the way to the Pole because ...
c .... were bitterly disappointed when ...
d They couldn't reach their base because ...
e .... disappeared in the Arctic when ...

GUIDED WRITING

Sentence linking
Personal letters

1 Look at Jenny's letter. These sentences are from the letter. What words has Jenny used to link the sentences?

I'm sorry I haven't written for a long time.
I've been away.
I was studying German at the university in Hamburg.
I had a great time.
Guess what, I had an accident.
I arrived.
I was crossing the street one day.
A cyclist ran into me.
It was all my fault.
I had forgotten that in Germany they drive on the right.
It wasn't a serious accident.
I was out there.
I visited lots of places.
I went to Denmark and Poland.
I got back last Friday.
I've been back about a week now.
I haven't done much.
I got back.
I've been having a rest.

20 Camberwell Drive
London SE20 7GH
5 June

Dear Fran

I'm sorry I haven't written for a long time, but I've been away. I was studying German at the university in Hamburg and I had a great time, but guess what, I had an accident soon after I arrived. When I was crossing the street one day, a cyclist ran into me. It was all my fault, because I had forgotten that in Germany they drive on the right. Luckily it wasn't a serious accident. While I was out there, I visited lots of places. I also went to Denmark and Poland. I got back last Friday, so I've been back about a week now. I haven't done much since I got back, as I've been having a rest.
I hope you're fine.
Bye for now,

Love,
Jenny

2 Look at the letter again and answer these questions.

a Which of these does the letter include?

- her address
- Fran's address
- the date
- Jenny's full name
- her signature

b What expressions does Jenny use to:

- start the letter?
- end the letter?

3 Choose one of the sets of information in Interaction Exercise 3. Write a letter to Jenny about the trip. Use your ideas from Exercises 1 and 2 above.

---- optional activity ----

Project suggestion

4 Find out as much as possible about a famous explorer. Write about him/her. Illustrate your project with maps and pictures.

▶ Pronunciation: page 110

Learning *diary* 2

What have you learnt in this unit?

A Do the self-check in the Workbook.

B Look back at the first page of this unit. What words have you looked up in a dictionary? Were you able to find the words easily?

Complete your Learning diary.

Learning objectives

Learning preview: Using a dictionary: 2

Victoria Road: Talking about the future ▶ 3.1–4

Language work: Expressing the future: 'will', 'going to', present continuous ▶ 3.1–4

Listening: Talking about work
Reduced relative clauses ▶ 3.5

Interaction: Talking about likes and dislikes
Gerunds ▶ 3.6

Reading: Giving advice
'if' clauses (1) ▶ 3.2

Guided writing: Choosing the correct tense
Your future

3 ambitions

Q Learning preview: *Using a dictionary: 2*

We usually use a dictionary to find or check meanings, but a dictionary gives a lot of other information, too.

1 What information can a dictionary give?

2 Find this information in the dictionary extract on pages 108–9. Use the notes around the dictionary page to help you.

  a There are two ways of pronouncing **financial**. What are they?

  b Which is the correct spelling: **faund** or **found**?

  c What is unusual about verbs with the noun **firm**?

  d What is the opposite of 'a **fine** pencil'?

  e Is **fir-cone** countable or uncountable?

  f What do Americans call **the fire brigade**?

  g Why should you be careful in using the expression **to finish somebody off**?

3 Make a list of things that you can use a dictionary for.

We can use a dictionary for:

checking spellings

Terry joins the band

1 What do you remember? What happened in the last part of the story? Look back at pages 18 and 19. Check your ideas.

2 Look at the pictures in this episode.

a Why are Rosie and Terry in the shop?
b Who do they see?
c What is Rosie worried about?
d Why are Dan and Kim arguing?
e What is happening in May?
f What is Dan's dream?

Picture 1:
Rosy: Welcome to the band, Terry. Your friend Shirley certainly taught you well. But that old acoustic guitar won't be any good. You'll have to get some decent electric equipment.
Terry: Yes, I know. I'll go and see about it this week.
Rosy: I'll come with you, if you like.

Picture 2:
Terry: Hey, look! There's Vince and Andrea in the street.
Rosy: Oh, yes. They always seem to be together. They're very fond of each other, aren't they?

Picture 3:
Rosy: I've got a funny feeling that something's going to happen there. And Kim isn't going to like it.

3 🎧 Listen and follow in your book.

Rosy Welcome to the band, Terry. Your friend Shirley certainly taught you well. But that old acoustic guitar won't be any good. You'll have to get some decent electric equipment.

Terry Yes, I know. I'll go and see about it this week.

Rosy I'll come with you, if you like. Will Thursday be OK for you – about four?

Thursday afternoon

Terry How much is all this lot going to cost, Rosy?

Rosy Don't worry. Ron will probably give you a discount. And it will be worth it.

Terry Hey, look! There's Vince and Andrea in the street.

Rosy Oh, yes. They always seem to be together. They're very fond of each other, aren't they?

Terry Yes, they get on very well together.

Rosy A bit too well, if you ask me. I've got a funny feeling that something's going to happen there. And Kim isn't going to like it.

VICTORIA ROAD

Panel 4:

Dan: Oh, yes. That was much better. That's the sound that we've been looking for. It's a pity we only had a singer for the last two numbers.

Kim: All right, Dan. I told you I missed the bus. Anyway, I'm going to buy a car next week, so I won't be late ever again.

Panel 5:

Rosy: We're playing a gig in a couple of weeks' time. It's at the leisure centre. It'll be our first really big performance.

Dan: Yes and who knows? Perhaps there'll be a recording agent in the audience and he'll offer us a big contract. We'll be on 'Top of the Pops' and then …

Panel 6:

Vince: Come on, Dan. We aren't playing at Wembley Stadium in May. We're doing a gig at the local leisure centre.

Dan: Don't be so sceptical, Vince. You've got to have a dream. If we can get our new sound together, the sky's the limit.

A few months later

Dan Oh, yes. That was much better. That's the sound that we've been looking for. It's a pity we only had a singer for the last two numbers.

Kim All right, Dan. I told you I missed the bus. Anyway, I'm going to buy a car next week, so I won't be late ever again.

Dan I'll believe that when I see it.

Rosy All right, you two. Now, we'll need to arrange some extra practice sessions if we want to be good for the May do.

Terry The May do? What's happening in May?

Rosy Don't you remember? We're playing a gig in a couple of weeks' time. It's at the leisure centre. It'll be our first really big performance.

Dan Yes and who knows? Perhaps there'll be a recording agent in the audience and he'll offer us a big contract. We'll be on 'Top of the Pops' and then …

Vince Come on, Dan. We aren't playing at Wembley Stadium in May. We're doing a gig at the local leisure centre.

Dan Don't be so sceptical, Vince. You've got to have a dream. If we can get our new sound together, the sky's the limit.

What do you think?

- Why is Rosy worried about Vince and Andrea?
- Who is right about the 'dream', Vince or Dan?

4 Right, Wrong or Don't know?

		✓	✗	?
a	Ron joins the band.	☐	☐	☐
b	Terry's equipment isn't very expensive.	☐	☐	☐
c	Rosy thinks that Vince and Andrea are falling in love.	☐	☐	☐
d	Kim was late for the practice session.	☐	☐	☐
e	The band has played at the leisure centre dances before.	☐	☐	☐
f	There will be a recording agent at the gig in May.	☐	☐	☐

Useful expressions

5 How do you say these expressions in your language? Do you know any other English expressions with a similar meaning?

I'll go and see about it.

They're very fond of each other.

They get on (very) well together.

Who knows?

if you ask me

The sky's the limit.

---

optional activities

LANGUAGE USE

6 Here are some utterances from the story where the speakers don't say exactly what they mean. What do they really mean?

- How much is all this lot going to cost, Rosy?
- I've got a funny feeling that something's going to happen there. And Kim isn't going to like it.
- It's a pity we only had a singer for the last two numbers.
- I'll believe that when I see it.

7 a 🎧 Close your book. Listen again.

b Work in pairs. One person is Vince, Terry and Kim. One is Rosy and Dan. Read the dialogue.

FOLLOW UP

8 Copy and complete these sentences.

a .... bought a new guitar.
b .... went to the music shop with Terry.
c .... works at the music shop.
d .... spend a lot of time together.
e .... was annoyed with Kim.
f .... is going to buy a car.
g .... thinks that the band will be famous.
h .... is sceptical about Dan's dream.

LANGUAGE WORK

Expressing the future ▶ 3.1–4

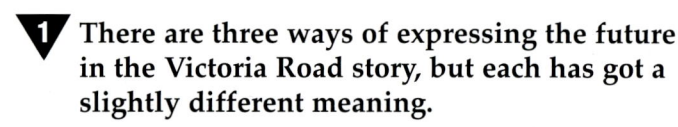

1 There are three ways of expressing the future in the Victoria Road story, but each has got a slightly different meaning.

a Copy the chart on the opposite page.

b Write one of the following at the top of the correct column.

the present continuous + future time expression
will + infinitive
going to + infinitive

c For each way of expressing the future, find examples in the Victoria Road story of a statement, a negative and a question. Write them in your chart.

2 Look at Exercises 3, 4 and 5.

a Which of the three ways of expressing the future is the most appropriate for each one?

b Why?

3 These are things that the Victoria Road characters have decided to do next week. Use the cues to make sentences.

A Vince and Terry/practise some of the numbers
B Kim/buy a car
C Terry/look for a job
D Rosy and Kim/see about a new microphone
E Andrea/take an exam
F Dan/get some new drumsticks

4 Rosy wants to have another practice session, but there are problems, because everyone already has arrangements for next week.

a Use the cues. Say what each person is doing.

A Vince and Kim/go to a pop concert/Monday
B Terry/meet his friend Shirley/Tuesday
C Vince and Dan/play football/Wednesday
D Kim/work late/Thursday
E Rosy and Dan/go to a party/Friday
F Terry/take Andrea out/Saturday

b Make the group's conversation. Ask and answer.

Example
What about (Monday)?
No. I (We) can't make (Monday), because I (we) ...

Form	....	....	....
Meaning	a general or indefinite future event	an intended or definite future event	an arrangement for a particular time in the future
Positive	....	....	....
Negative	....	....	....
Question	....	....	....

5 Terry has never done a gig before. Kim is telling him what will probably happen. Complete their conversation. Use these verbs.

get   be   enjoy   get changed
take   have   unload
play   practise need

Kim Rosy .... the equipment in her van, I suppose. We .... it and then we .... probably .... a few numbers.

Terry What should we wear?

Kim You can wear what you want. You .... some old clothes for setting up the equipment. You .... probably .... quite dirty doing that. We .... after the practice session.

Terry .... we .... on stage all evening?

Kim No. We .... for a couple of hours, I imagine. Then they .... a disco. Don't worry. You .... it.

— optional activities —

6 What about your future?

a Write:
- three things that you are going to do today
- three arrangements that you have made for next week
- three things that you think will happen before your next birthday

b Compare your answers with a partner.

FOLLOW UP

7 Look at the chart you made in Exercise 1. Write a sentence about your life in each space.

Examples
I think I'll go to university.
I won't be very tall.
Will I be famous?

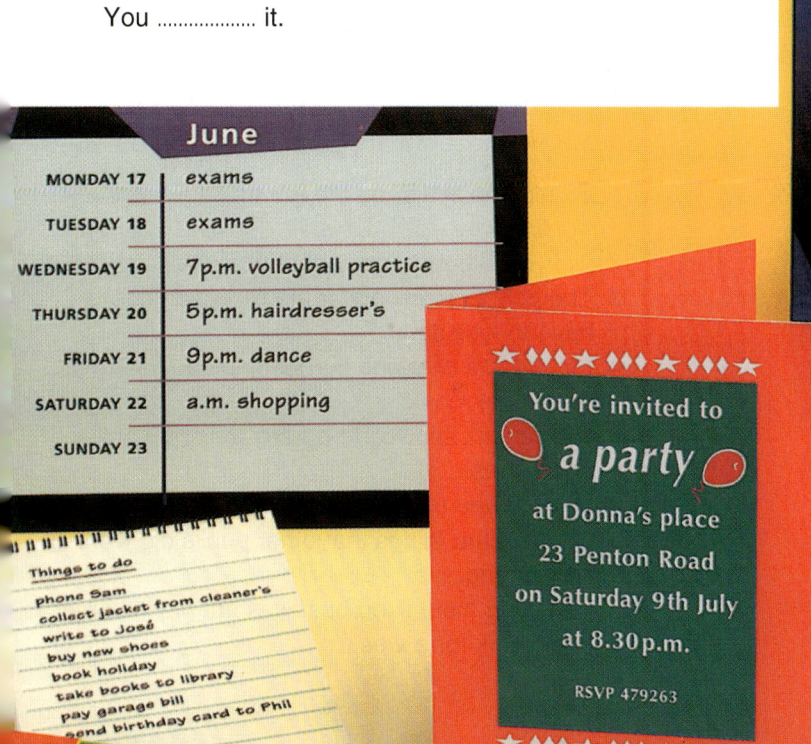

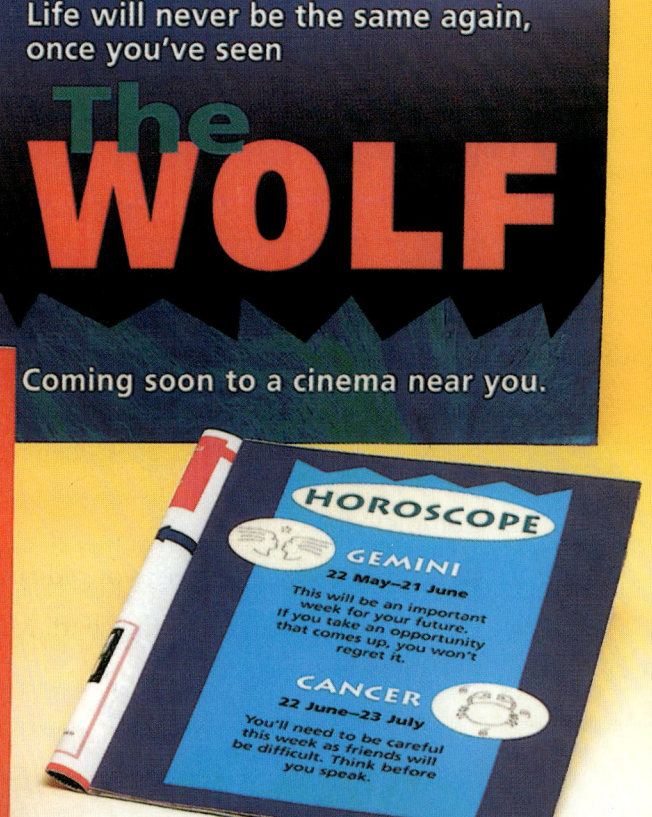

LISTENING

Work

1 Read the text and answer the questions.

a What school do the girls and boys go to?
b What have they been doing?
c What is work experience for?

The pupils in year 11 of Sutton High School haven't been at school for the last two weeks. They've been doing work experience. They've been working in factories, shops, banks, hotels and other local workplaces. Work experience shows young people what life is like in the world of work, and it can also help them to choose a career. Here, some of the pupils are talking about their experiences.

2 Look at the pictures.

a In what kinds of places are the people working?
b 🔊 Listen. Where did Carol and Mike work?

3 Copy this chart.

	Carol	Mike
Where?		
What things did they do?		
What did they enjoy?		
What didn't they enjoy?		
Would they like to do the job?		
Why?/Why not?		

a Complete the chart.
b 🔊 Listen again and check your ideas.
c Work with a partner. Use the chart. Make the dialogues.

Reduced relative clauses

▶ 3.5

4 Look at these sentences.

I unpacked the new clothes that came in.
I did all the jobs shop assistants do.

a Both of these sentences contain relative clauses. Find them.

b What is different about the second sentence?

c We can leave out the relative pronoun, but only when the pronoun is the object of the relative clause. Look at these sentences. Remove the relative pronouns where possible.

1 Would you like to do the job that you did all the time?
2 Did you like the people that you met?
3 The people that work at the reception desk have to look smart.
4 I found lots of things that people had left in their hotel rooms.
5 We weren't allowed to do any jobs that are dangerous.
6 Jeff showed me all the jobs that I had to do.
7 Some of the things that other pupils did were very boring.
8 The thing that I liked best was not having any homework for a week.

INTERACTION

Gerunds: revision ▶ 3.6

1 What kind of job would you like to do?

a Ask and answer with a partner. Use the cues and find out what he/she likes.

Example
Do you like wearing a uniform?
Yes, I do. / No, I don't.

wear a uniform	work at night	be on stage
speak English	travel	meet people
work with animals	work outdoors	work with children
	make things	
get up early	study	use computers
get dirty	handle money	

b Find out two more things that your partner likes and two that he/she doesn't like.

c Write down what you have found out.

Example
My partner likes ...   He/She doesn't like ...

2 Choose six of the things in Exercise 1a. Think of a job where you would have to do each one. Try to find a different job for each thing. Use a dictionary to help you.

Example
wear a uniform: police officer, soldier

3 Imagine you could do any job at all for work experience.

Example
pilot, actor, prime minister, model, farmer

a How would you answer the questions in Listening Exercise 3 for your chosen job?

b You have just been doing your job for a week. Work with a partner. Make the interview about it.

— optional activity —

FOLLOW UP

4 Choose five jobs. Say whether you could or couldn't do each job and why. Use the cues in Exercise 1.

Example
I could be a pilot, because I like travelling and wearing a uniform. However, I don't like getting up early, and I wouldn't like working at night.

— optional activities —

5 Discussion points

a What do you think of Carol and Mike's experience?

b Do you have work experience in your country?

c Where would you like to do work experience?

d Have you ever done a regular job? What was it like?

FOLLOW UP

6 Use the information in your chart in Exercise 3. Summarise what Carol and Mike said.

Example
Carol worked ... . For the first two days she ... . After that she ... . She enjoyed ..., but she didn't enjoy ... . She would(n't) like to ..., because ...

READING

1 Look quickly at the text.
  a What is it about?
  b Where do you think it is from?

> Millions of kids dream about being a pop star and many of them form groups, but only a handful will make it to the top. If you want to hit the big time, you'll have to work hard and get the basics right.

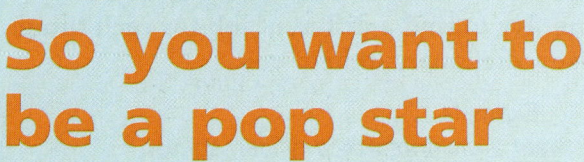

So you want to be a pop star

First of all, if you want to make a decent sound, you'll need some decent equipment. Don't be too ambitious. The more gear you've got, the more things can go wrong. Modern amplifiers and loudspeakers are very powerful, so you don't really need a lot. But always buy the best gear that you can afford.

Buying good quality equipment will be a waste of money if you don't look after it. Always keep an instrument in its case, when you aren't using it, and don't leave equipment near a radiator or in a hot car. (It's not a good idea to leave stuff in a car anyway, as someone could nick it.) Never, never, never stand a drink on top of your amp or speaker. If it gets knocked over, a few hundred pounds (and probably you, too) will go up in smoke.

You'll find it easier to look after equipment properly if you've got some transport, so a good, reliable set of wheels is a must. A van is best, because it's cheaper and more convenient.

Of course, just having good equipment won't make a good sound. It's the band members who really make the band. Here the most important thing is to keep everyone together and avoid arguments. All the band members must want to play the same kind of music. If the drummer is into heavy metal and the singer likes mainstream pop, you'll have problems sooner or later.

You can't afford a weak member of the group. It will cause arguments if someone can't play as well as the others. And you don't want someone who constantly 'can't make it this week'. It will be better for everyone if you get rid of any weak members as soon as possible.

Lastly, keep romance out of the band. People do silly things when they're in love and even sillier things when they're breaking up. You need to put your energy into your music, not into handling emotional problems.

2
Look at the text again. Which of these topics does it give advice about?

finding a manager
looking after equipment
keeping the band together
choosing songs
setting up a gig
emotional relationships
choosing a name
transport
finding an image
choosing equipment

3
Look at the topics in Exercise 2.

a Read the text more carefully. Make a list of Dos and Don'ts for each topic.

b Which of the Dos and Don'ts are Vince's group following? Write **Yes, No** or **Don't know** next to each item in your list. Find evidence in the story so far to justify your answers.

---
optional activity

W O R D   W O R K

4
There are a lot of informal expressions in the text.

a Match the items in column A with the meanings in column B.

A	B
go up in smoke	a few
gear	an amplifier
hit the big time	a loudspeaker
a speaker	a vehicle
nick	be lost
kids	steal
is into	things
a must	become a star
breaking up	young people
a set of wheels	ending a relationship
a handful	is a fan of
an amp	equipment
stuff	necessary

b Find another expression which means 'to become a star'.

'if' clauses (1) ▶ 3.2

5
Look at these sentences from the text.

1 ... if you .... to make a decent sound, you .... some decent equipment.

2 Buying good quality equipment .... a waste of money if you .... it.

a Copy and complete them.

b What tense is used in:
  • the **if** clause?   • the main clause?

c Match the cues in A and B to make sentences with **if** clauses.

  A you / want to reach the top
     more things / go wrong
     you / leave a guitar near a radiator
     you / stand a drink on your amp
     you / have a weak member of the group
     someone / not good enough
     it / cause problems

  B it / cause arguments
     you / damage it
     you / have to get rid of them
     you / need to work hard
     a romance in the group / break up
     you / have a lot of gear
     it / get knocked over

---
optional activities

6
Discussion points

a Which bit of advice is the most important? Do you disagree with any of the advice? What further advice would you give?

b Do you dream about being a pop star? What are your ambitions?

FOLLOW UP

7
Copy and complete these sentences with items from column A of Exercise 4.

a Somebody's .... my pen.
b I'm really .... computer games.
c Kim's going to get ....
d Terry's bought some decent ....
e He's bought a guitar, ... and a ....
f Only .... of people came to the gig.

GUIDED WRITING

Form and meaning

1 Look at Exercise 2 below.

a Match these topics to the correct paragraphs.
- arrangements
- plans
- predictions

b Which of these language forms will you use in each paragraph? Why?
- 'will'
- 'going to'
- the present continuous

Your future

2 What does the future hold for you? Write about your future. Use this pattern.

My future

When I grow up, I .... (job/ambitions), because I like .... and I'm good at .... So when I leave school, I (How do you intend to get the qualifications and experience?)

In the future I think that the world .... (What will the world be like?). Scientists .... (What will scientists invent? How will these inventions change life?). People .... (What will daily life be like?). But if .... I (don't) think .... (possible problems).

What does the immediate future hold for me? Well, first of all, ... and then (any arrangements you have for the week/month/year).

--- optional activity ---

Project suggestion

3 Illustrate your text with photographs, pictures and diagrams.

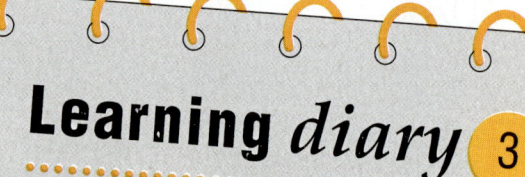

Learning *diary* 3

What have you learnt in this unit?

A Do the self-check in the Workbook.

B Look back at the first page of this unit. What have you used a dictionary for in this unit?

Complete your Learning diary.

▶ Pronunciation: page 111

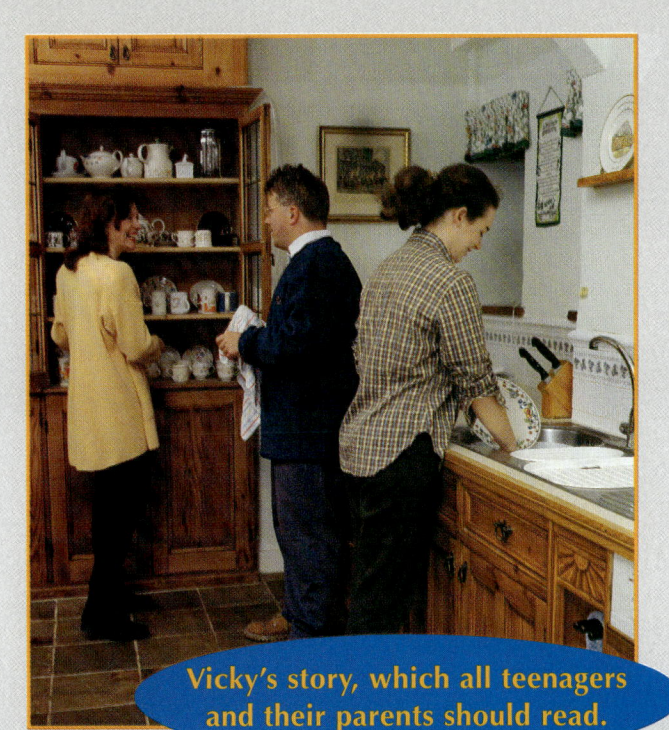

revision 4

1 reading skills tenses

1 Look at the title, the pictures and the captions.

   a Who is the girl?

   b What do you think happened to her?

2 Look at these names. Read the text. What part did each person play in the story?

1	Vicky Samson	A	telephoned the police.
2	Mrs Samson	B	was decorating a Christmas tree.
3	Sharon Robinson	C	argued with Vicky a lot.
4	Mr Robinson	D	went to collect Vicky.
5	Mrs Robinson	E	ran away from home.
6	Mr Samson	F	found Vicky.

Vicky's story, which all teenagers and their parents should read.

No place like home

Today Vicky Samson came home from school at four o'clock. She watched TV for half an hour. Then she did her homework. She's working hard at the moment, because she's got exams soon. After dinner, while she was helping with the washing up, she talked to her parents about a problem she has been having at school.

'I can't believe it. Four months ago I was living in a cardboard box under a railway bridge in London.'

It was a normal day, but it was the kind of day that makes Vicky (and her parents) very happy. 'I can't believe it,' says Vicky. 'Four months ago I was living in a cardboard box under a railway bridge in London.'

Last October Vicky had run away from home. How did it all start? 'I hated school. We always had so much work to do and I didn't see the point of it all. My mum didn't understand. We only spoke to each other when we were arguing. One day I just couldn't stand it any more.'

On that October day, Vicky didn't go to school. She went to the station and caught the train to London. 'At first it was really exciting. There were all the bright lights, theatres and shops and some really interesting people. I had to sleep on the streets, but I didn't mind. I was free – no school, no homework, no parents.'

But soon there was no food and no money either. Vicky was cold, hungry and miserable, but she survived until one night about a week before Christmas. 'I was walking down a street, when I looked into someone's front window. There was a girl there, just like me. She was decorating a Christmas tree. I thought "If I was at home, I'd be decorating our tree now." Then I couldn't help it. I just sat down on the pavement and cried and cried.'

Luckily for Vicky, the man who lived at the house, Mr Robinson, came home while she was sitting there. He took Vicky into the house and Mrs Robinson gave her something to eat. 'They were so kind. I told them my whole story. They offered to pay for my ticket home, but I didn't want that. I thought my parents would be angry.'

But the next day she was back home. While Vicky was at their house, Mrs Robinson went next door and telephoned the police in Birmingham. Three hours later, Vicky's father arrived to collect her.

'It was the best Christmas present I'd ever had', said Mrs Samson.

3 Read the text in more detail. Answer these questions.

a Why did Vicky run away from home?
b How did she do it?
c How did she feel when she first arrived in London?
d What made her want to go home?
e When did she go home?
f How did she get home?
g How has life changed since then?

--- optional activity ---

4 Discussion points

a Was Vicky right to run away?
b What did her parents think when she disappeared?
c Did the Robinsons do the right thing?

5 Vicky is telling Mr Robinson her story. Put the verbs in brackets into the correct tense. Choose from this list:

- the past simple
- the past continuous
- the past perfect
- the present perfect
- the present perfect continuous

Mr Robinson How long have you been in London, Vicky?

Vicky I .... (be) in London since October. Everything .... (be) fine at first. I .... (save) some money to bring with me. But then somebody .... (nick) my purse. I got a job in a restaurant, but that .... (not last) very long, because the restaurant closed down. Since then I .... (live) under a railway bridge. And the weather .... (become) very cold lately. When I looked through your window, Sharon .... (decorate) the Christmas tree. When I .... (see) her, I .... (start) crying. You see, I .... always .... (help) to do our tree at home. Oh, I hope my parents .... (not worry) about me too much.

6 What is Vicky's life like now?

a Correct these sentences.

1 Vicky come home at 4 o'clock every day.
2 She not watch TV for more than half an hour.
3 She are happy these days.
4 Her parents talks to her about problems.
5 They doesn't argues very much.

b Rewrite the sentences with these words.

usually   normally   always   often   usually

c Look at the picture at the top of page 37. Use these cues and write sentences to say what the people are doing.

Vicky	work in the kitchen
Vicky's mother	wash up
Vicky's father	put things in the cupboard
Vicky and her parents	dry the dishes

7 What does the future hold for Vicky? Copy and complete the sentences with the verbs in brackets.

a This is what Vicky and her parents have decided.

1 Vicky .... some new clothes. (buy)
2 She .... hard at school. (work)
3 They .... a party. (have)

b Vicky has a lot of work to do.

1 If she .... her friends, they .... her with the work she missed. (ask/help)
2 She .... her exams if she .... hard. (pass/work)
3 If she .... her homework every day, she .... any problems. (do/not have)

c Here are some of her arrangements.

1 She .... an exam next month. (take)
2 In February Sharon Robinson .... for the weekend. (come)
3 At Easter Vicky and her parents .... on holiday. (go)

--- optional activity ---

8 Use your answers to Exercise 3. Write Vicky's story from her parents' point of view.

2 listening skills
gerunds
writing skills

Sons and daughters

1 You are going to hear part of a radio phone-in programme.

a Here are some things that people say in the programme. What do you think the programme is about?

1 Some things are too embarrassing to talk to your parents about.
2 My parents never have time to talk to me.
3 I can talk to my parents about anything.
4 My parents always treat me like a little child.

b ▭ Listen and check your ideas.

2 Here are the names of the speakers on the phone-in.

Cindy Wright   Stuart Whittaker
Fiona Smith   Ross Ball

a ▭ Listen again and match the numbers of the statements in Exercise 1 to the correct names.

b What examples do the speakers give to illustrate their points?

c Listen again and check your ideas.

— optional activities —

3 Discussion points

a Do you agree with the speakers? Why? Why not?

b If you were on the phone-in programme, what would you say?

FOLLOW UP

4 Write a summary of the phone-in programme and add your own views. Use your answers to Exercises 1–3.

Example
Fiona thinks that .... (Give Fiona's view.)
She says that her mother .... (Give Fiona's example.)

(Continue with the other speakers.)

I think that .... (Give your view.) *For example,* .... (Give an example of what you mean.)

> Sharon! Tidy this room at ONCE! Sharon? Sharon? I know you're in there somewhere.

> I said: Can you turn it DOWN?

— optional activity —

5 Write to the radio station.

a Suggest a topic for discussion on the phone-in programme. Give your reasons and your personal experience.

b Use this letter as a model.

> Dear Diana
>
> I think it would be a good idea to discuss talking to parents on your phone-in programme.
>
> I often want to talk to my parents, but I can't. They're always too busy. There's always something that's more important than talking to me.
>
> I know that a lot of my friends have got the same problem with their parents, so I'm sure that you would get lots of callers.
>
> I hope you like the idea.
>
> Yours,
> Ross Ball
> Ross Ball

3 project

Teenage life

What is it like to be a teenager today? Make a project about it.

1 Here are some things that you could research and write about. Can you think of any more?

- parents and family
- friends
- school
- interests/free time
- teenage rights
- problems/worries/concerns
- jobs
- drugs/alcohol/cigarettes
- advice for parents

2 How can you present your information? Here are some possible ideas. What would you need to do for these things?

- magazine articles
- surveys
- a problem page
- audio presentations or interviews
- a radio phone-in
- a video
- a poster

3 Follow this procedure.

a Discuss and choose topics.

b Decide how you will present your project.

c Divide the work among the members of the group.

d Individuals or pairs produce their part of the work.

e As a group discuss each contribution. Check and correct them.

f Find or produce any illustrations.

g Prepare your final project.

h Present your project.

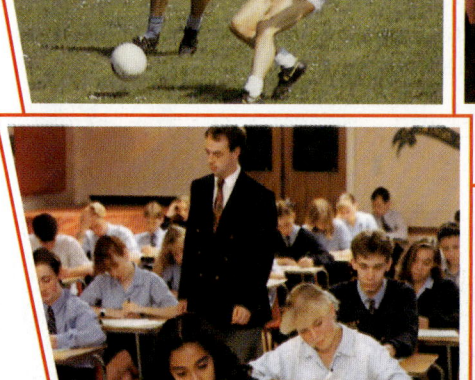

▶ Pronunciation: page 111

Learning *diary* 4

Look back through your Learning diary.

- What have you studied so far this year?
- How well do you know these things?
- Is there anything that you still don't understand?

Check in the Grammar reference and your vocabulary notebook. Make a list of things you need to revise.

5 motor mania

Learning objectives

Learning preview: Parts of speech

Victoria Road: Talking about the environment

Language work: The passive voice ▶5.1–2
'used to' ▶5.3

Listening: Understanding a description of a process
Modal verbs and the passive voice ▶5.1–2

Interaction: Writing a dialogue

Reading: Interpreting attitudes for and against
Tenses in the passive voice ▶5.1

Guided writing: Topic sentences

Learning preview: *Parts of speech*

1 It is very useful to know the different parts of speech. It can help you to use a dictionary or a grammar book more easily.

a Often you can tell a part of speech from its context. In this text there are some nonsense words. What parts of speech are they? Choose from this list.

verb   noun   adjective   adverb   preposition   pronoun   article   conjunction

> It was a **fingshal** day **vok** Jane was **poddling** in the garden. Suddenly **brak** a tree she saw a **crinch**. It was crying **shuffly**. Jane picked up the **crinch** and put it on a **kwit**. **Sujbo** the **crinch shrooed** and Jane felt **boggly fush**.

b What parts of speech are these words? Use the dictionary extract on pages 108–9 and find out.

finder   fine   fire   finish   fiord   finch

c Some of the words can be more than one part of speech. How is this indicated in the dictionary?

2 When you meet unknown words in this unit, first decide what part of speech they are. Does this help you to work out the meaning?

Kim buys a car

1 What do you remember? What happened in the last part of the story? Look back at pages 28 and 29. Check your ideas.

2 Look at the pictures. Complete the sentences with the correct subjects.

a .... is buying a car.

b .... is checking the car for her.

c .... would like to have a sports car.

d .... thinks that cars damage the environment.

e .... suggests going out in the car on Sunday.

f .... has promised to take Andrea out.

g .... suggests that they go to Stonehenge together.

3 Listen and follow in your book.

Saleswoman All our used cars are thoroughly tested by our mechanics, Mr Scott. Any worn tyres are replaced. The cars are cleaned inside. All the paintwork is checked and resprayed, if necessary. And it's polished, too, of course.

Mr Scott Well, I'll, er, just take it for a road test, if that's all right.

Later

Kim It was very nice of your dad to come and look at the car for me. I hope he didn't mind.

Vince Mind? He's never happier than when he's got his head under the bonnet of a car.

Terry Now, this is really smart. This is my idea of a car.

Vince Is it your idea of a price, too? Anyway, what do you want a wasteful thing like that for? Don't you know that cars are the biggest threat to the global environment, and the more powerful the engine, the greater the pollution?

Terry Well, thank you Professor Scott for that very interesting lecture. I suppose you think that we should all walk everywhere?

Vince It would be better for the environment if we did. People used to manage without cars.

Terry Oh, come on, Vince. People used to live in caves, too. And people used to die from smallpox. Haven't you ever heard of progress?

Kim No, Terry. I think Vince is right. We should all think about the environment.

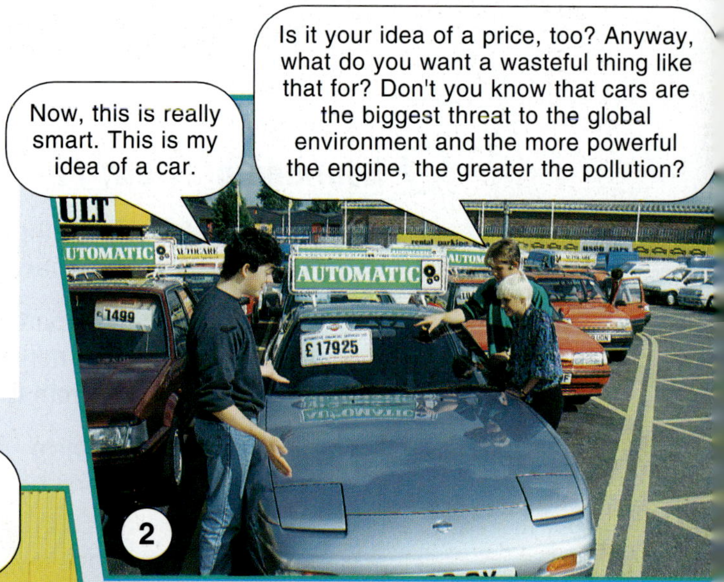

VICTORIA ROAD

Later

Kim Shall we go for a spin on Sunday, Vince? Somewhere out in the country.

Vince Oh, well, actually I … er … I promised Andrea that I'd take her to see Stonehenge on Sunday.

Kim Well, thanks for telling me. What about you, Terry? Do you fancy a day in the country?

Terry Sure, but why don't we make a foursome and all go to Stonehenge in your car, Kim?

Kim That's a good idea. There's no need to take two cars. Better for the environment, eh, Vince?

Well, thank you Professor Scott for that very interesting lecture. I suppose you think that we should all walk everywhere?

It would be better for the environment if we did. People used to manage without cars.

What do you think?

- Is Vince right about cars?
- How does he feel about the trip on Sunday?
- What does Kim think about Vince's arrangement for Sunday?

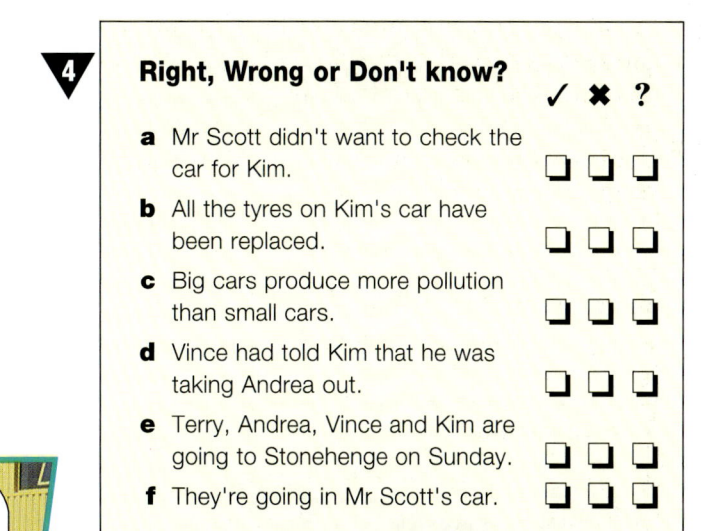

Right, Wrong or Don't know?   ✓ ✗ ?

a Mr Scott didn't want to check the car for Kim.

b All the tyres on Kim's car have been replaced.

c Big cars produce more pollution than small cars.

d Vince had told Kim that he was taking Andrea out.

e Terry, Andrea, Vince and Kim are going to Stonehenge on Sunday.

f They're going in Mr Scott's car.

Shall we go for a spin on Sunday, Vince? Somewhere out in the country.

Oh, well, actually I … er … I promised Andrea that I'd take her to see Stonehenge on Sunday.

Well, thanks for telling me. What about you, Terry? Do you fancy a day in the country?

Sure, but why don't we make a foursome and all go to Stonehenge in your car, Kim?

That's a good idea. There's no need to take two cars. Better for the environment, eh, Vince?

Useful expressions

5 How do you say these expressions in your language? Do you know any other English expressions with a similar meaning?

if that's all right

This is my idea of a car.

to go for a spin

out in the country

Thanks for telling me.

to make a foursome

— optional activities —

LANGUAGE USE

6 Look at the story again. Find examples of where people:
- make suggestions
- disagree or argue with someone.

7 a 📼 Close your book. Listen again.

b Work in groups of three. One person is Vince, one person is Terry and the saleswoman and one person is Kim and Mr Scott. Read the dialogue.

FOLLOW UP

8 Answer these questions.

a What is Kim doing?
b Why is Mr Scott at the garage with Kim?
c Why doesn't Mr Scott mind?
d What kind of car would Terry like?
e Why does Vince think that fast cars aren't a good idea?
f What does Kim want to do on Sunday?
g What had Vince planned to do on Sunday?

LANGUAGE WORK

The passive voice: revision

▶ 5.1–2

1 The sentences below are from the Victoria Road story on pages 42 and 43.

a Copy and complete them.

Any worn tyres ....

All the paintwork ....

The verbs in these sentences are in the passive voice. We normally use the passive when the action is more important than the person or thing that does it.

b Copy and complete this rule.

> To make the passive voice we use the verb _____ + the past participle.

c We can use an agent to show who or what does the action. Read what the saleswoman says. What word introduces the agent?

All our used cars are tested by our mechanics.

d Rewrite the saleswoman's sentence in the active voice. What happens to the subject and the agent?

2 Here are some important environmental problems. Write the sentences in the passive voice.

Example
The air in cities is polluted by vehicles.

1 Vehicles pollute the air in cities.
2 People waste too much energy.
3 Timber companies cut down rainforests.
4 Poachers hunt rare animals.
5 Acid rain destroys forests.
6 Power stations produce greenhouse gases.
7 Oil pollutes the sea.
8 Fishermen catch too much fish.

— optional activity —

3 Discuss these questions.

a What do you know about any of the problems in Exercise 2?
b Which do you think are the most important?
c What can we do about the problems?

Recycling glass

4 Look at the pictures.

a Match the pictures to the correct cues.

b Use the cues. Describe how glass is recycled.

  Example
  Old bottles are taken to a bottle bank.

c Do you recycle glass or other materials? How does recycling help?

1. old bottles/take to a bottle bank
2. bottle bank/collect/lorry
3. it/take/to a recycling plant
4. bottles/crush/into small pieces
5. tops and labels/remove
6. crushed bottles/mix/with new materials
7. mixture/heat/to make new glass
8. new bottles/make

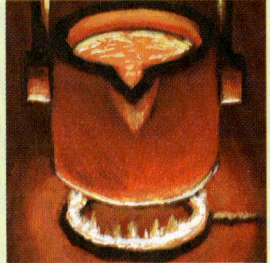

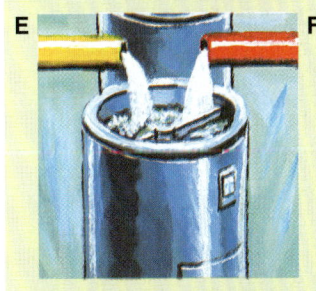

'used to' ▶ 5.3

5 The sentences below are from the Victoria Road story on pages 42 and 43.

a Copy and complete them.

  People .... without cars.

  People .... in caves.

  This means that people did these things in the past but they don't do them any more.

b **used to** is the same for all subjects.

  Examples
  We used to live in London.
  She used to smoke.

c We make questions like this.

  Where *did you use to* live?
  Did you use to have a teddy bear when you were a child?

6 How has your life changed?

a Write down these things.

- something you used to do in your free time
- a favourite toy or pet you used to have
- what you used to look like
- a song you used to like
- a TV programme you used to watch every day
- something you used to hate
- something you used to be afraid of

b Now work in pairs. Ask your partner questions about the things in Exercise 6a. Use these expressions.

  What did you use to ...?
  Did you use to ...?

  Example
  A *What did you use to do in your free time?*
  B *I used to go to dance classes, but I don't now. What about you?*
  A *I used to ...*

— optional activity —

FOLLOW UP

7 Write your answers to Exercise 4b.

LISTENING

The most unpopular men in London

1 Read the paragraph below and find the answers to these questions. Use the list of irregular verbs on page 126 to help you if necessary.

a What do people do to John and Dave?
b What is John and Dave's job?

It's half past eight in the morning and John Punch is starting his day's work. Before he finishes, he and his mate, Dave Wilson, will be shouted at, argued with and sworn at. But that's all in a day's work for two of the most unpopular men in London. For John and Dave are a tow-away team. They lift cars that have been illegally parked and take them away to the car pound.

2 What happens when a car is towed away? Listen and put these events in the correct order.

A A yellow sticker is placed on the windscreen.
B The car is taken to the pound.
C The car is seen by a police officer or a traffic warden.
D The car is lifted onto a lorry.
E The motorist has to pay a fine to get the car back.
F The sticker is seen by a tow-away team.
G A car is illegally parked by a motorist.

3 Look at these questions.

a Choose the correct answers.
b Listen again and check your ideas.

1 Which of these kinds of illegal parking are mentioned?

- on double yellow lines
- on zebra crossings
- on bends
- double parked

2 How long do John and Dave usually take to remove a vehicle?

- 1 minute
- 3 minutes
- 5 minutes
- 10 minutes

3 What happens if the owner arrives before the car has been lifted?

- The car is still taken to the pound.
- The motorist has to pay a fine.
- The motorist is allowed to drive it away.

4 How much does it cost to get a car out of the pound?

- £100
- £101
- £110

5 Who might the car be dropped for?

- a pregnant woman
- an old person
- someone who's in a hurry
- a mother with a lot of children

— optional activity —

4 How do people feel about John and Dave?

a What sort of things do people do if they see their car being lifted?
b Why does John think that his job is important?

46

Modal verbs + passive ▶ 5.1

5 Look at these sentences from the tape.

a Complete them, using the verbs in brackets.

A Any car with a yellow sticker ....
(can/tow away)

B If it's a pregnant woman or a mother with lots of kids, the car .... (might/drop)

C At the pound, a fee of £101 .... to get the car back again. (must/pay)

D Cars .... on bends. (shouldn't/park)

b Listen again and check your answers.

c Complete this rule.

> When we use a modal verb with the passive, the pattern is:
> _____ + _____ + past participle.

--- optional activities ---

6 Discussion points
- What do you think about John and Dave's job?
- Are there similar people in your town?
- Would you like to do their job?
- Do you think the job is necessary?
- What would happen if there were no tow-away teams?

FOLLOW UP

7 Write about John and Dave's job.
- Describe what they do.
- Say how they feel about their job.
- Give some examples of things that happen to them.

INTERACTION

A parking incident

1 Work in groups. Write a dialogue about a parking incident.

a Read this information.

> A car is double parked and a sticker has been put on it. A tow-away team arrives to remove the car. When the car is off the ground, the motorist returns. The motorist tries to persuade the tow-away team to put the car down.

b Provide an ending for the story.

c Write the dialogue. Use these expressions.

> What are you doing with my car?
> Where are you taking it?
> You can't do that.
> Put it down at once.
> I couldn't find anywhere to park.
> I'm in a hurry.
> It's only been here five minutes.
> I had a lot of things to carry.
>
> I'm sorry, but ...
> Cars shouldn't be ...
> It's dangerous, because ...
> I'm afraid that's your problem.
> You'll have to ...
> We aren't allowed to ...

2 Act your play.

--- optional activity ---

FOLLOW UP

3 The tow-away team had to write a report on the incident.

a Look at the structure of their report below. Think which tenses you will need. Did things happen at the same time? Had some things happened before the team arrived?

b Write the report.

> At quarter past ten this morning we were going along the High Street, when we saw ...
> A yellow sticker ..., because ...
> We stopped and ...
> While we ...
> He/she ... But, we ...
> (Provide a conclusion.)

READING

Auto-crazy

1 Look at the texts and the picture.

a What are they all about?

b The texts are all extracts from magazine articles. Here are the titles of the articles. Look quickly at the texts and match the titles to the correct texts.

The dream machine
A brief history of the car
The greatest polluter of all
The human cost of the car
Going nowhere fast

1 The Department of Transport announced last week that deaths on Britain's roads had fallen. Good news? Well, it still means that over four and a half thousand people die on the roads every year. Worldwide, more than a quarter of a million people are killed in car accidents and four times as many are injured.

2 Most of the pollution in cities is caused by cars and other vehicles. Every time your car is used, dangerous chemicals like carbon monoxide and nitrogen oxide are pumped into the atmosphere.

But somebody's air or water had been polluted by your car even before it reached the road. Your car contains about five and a half pounds of plastic in the seats, the dashboard, the cables and so on. For each pound of plastic, two pounds of toxic chemicals were produced and these have been dumped somewhere.

Eventually your car will be scrapped and more pollution will be caused. If we cared about the environment, most of the materials would be recycled. Some of the metal will be, but the tyres, the battery, and all the plastic will be burnt or buried in the ground. So either the air or the land will be polluted again.

3 Films have been made about it. Songs have been written about it. It's been called the symbol of the twentieth century. What is it? It's the car.

A car is more than just a piece of machinery. A car is freedom. You can travel when you want. And take as much luggage as you like. Another bag? OK. Just put it in the boot.

Get behind the steering wheel of a car and you leave the ordinary world behind. As you speed along the open road with the wind in your hair, you can be anyone you want.

4 The internal combustion engine was invented by Karl-Friedrich Benz in Germany in 1885. But the car remained little more than a toy for the rich until 1913, when the American, Henry Ford, set up the world's first assembly line. Ford's factory produced cars that were cheap enough for the ordinary worker to buy. Today there are about 400 million cars in the world and every day another 100,000 cars roll off the world's assembly lines.

Millions of people work in the automobile and oil industries and our whole way of life is now built around cars. New towns and suburbs are so large that life would be impossible without a car.

5 I bought a new car recently – 24 valve, 2 litre engine. It can accelerate from 0 to 60 mph in less than 8 seconds. I thought about that yesterday, as I sat in a traffic jam on the motorway.

2 A lot of information is given in the texts. Some of it is in favour of the car, some is against and some is neutral.

a Make a chart like this.

for	against	neutral

b Read the texts again. Complete your chart.

c Can you add any more information to your chart?

3 Say whether these statements are true or false according to the texts.

a Over a million people are injured on the world's roads each year.
b Cars produce carbon monoxide.
c The plastic in an average car produces eleven pounds of toxic by-products.
d None of the materials in a modern car are recycled.
e Forty million new cars are produced every year.
f People who live in new towns and suburbs need a car.
g The car is the symbol of the twentieth century.

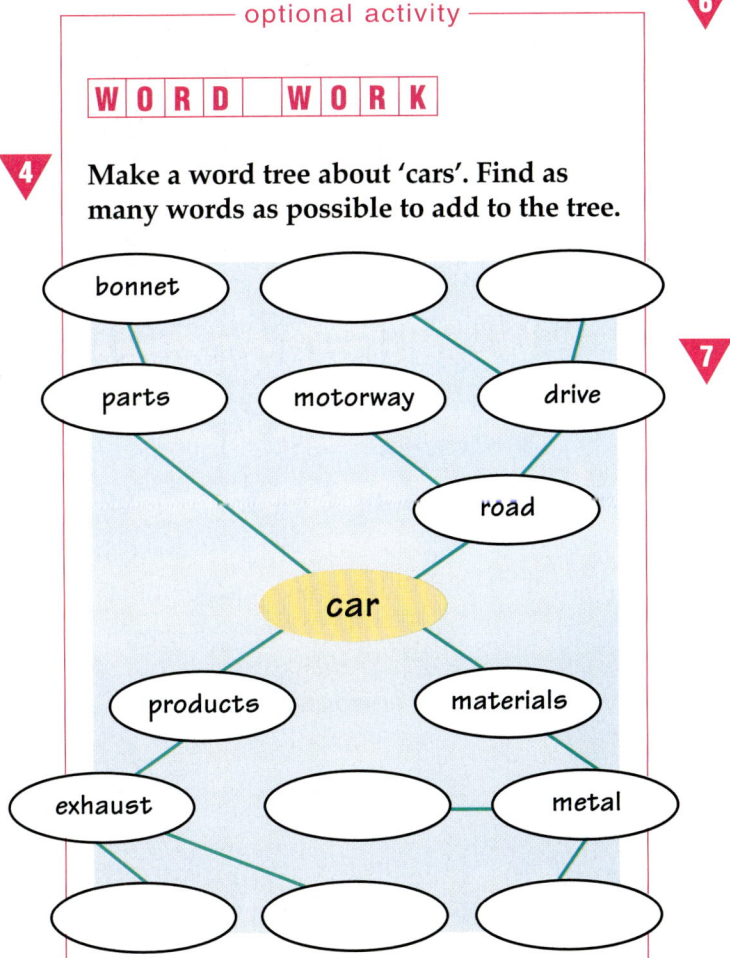

--- optional activity ---

W O R D   W O R K

4 Make a word tree about 'cars'. Find as many words as possible to add to the tree.

(word tree with: bonnet, parts, motorway, drive, road, car, products, materials, exhaust, metal)

Tenses in the passive voice ▶ 5.1

5 Look at these sentences from one of the texts.

A Every time your car .... , dangerous chemicals like carbon monoxide and nitrogen oxide .... into the atmosphere.

B But somebody's air or water .... by your car even before it reached the road.

C For each pound of plastic, two pounds of toxic chemicals .... and these .... somewhere.

D Eventually your car ....

E If we cared about the environment, most of the materials ....

a Copy and complete the sentences.

b How do we make different tenses in the passive voice? Which part of the verb changes?

--- optional activities ---

6 Discussion points

a What should be done to solve some of the problems described in the texts?

b If you had a car, would you be prepared to give it up or limit its use in order to help the environment?

FOLLOW UP

7 How do cars affect your life? Write down some information about these things.

a Look at your local neighbourhood. What effects do cars have on it? Consider parking, pollution, congestion, safety, services that cars need.

b What do people in your family use cars for? How much do they spend on cars? What would their life be like without a car?

GUIDED WRITING

Topic sentences

1 In Units 1 and 3 you looked at the topics of paragraphs. Paragraphs often have a sentence that tells us the topic. This is called the topic sentence. The other sentences in the paragraph add more details.

a Look at text 2 on page 48. What is the topic of each paragraph?

b Find a topic sentence for each paragraph.

c Where do you usually find the topic sentence?

d If you put all the topic sentences together they normally make a summary of the text. Try this with your sentences.

e What other details are added to each paragraph?

Cars

2 Write an essay called 'The car: dream machine or nightmare?' Use the information from your chart in Exercise 2 on page 49. Your essay should have the following structure.

Modern society couldn't exist without the car. (Give some ways in which we depend on cars).
In fact, our lives are organized around cars. (Give some ways in which cars determine our lifestyle, cities, etc.)

The car brings a lot of benefits. (Give some of the benefits that cars bring.)

However, we pay a heavy price for these benefits. (Give some of the disadvantages of cars.)

As more and more people get cars, the problems will increase, so we must change our attitude towards cars. (Give some ways in which we can reduce the problems that cars cause.)

---- optional activity ----

Project suggestion

3 Illustrate your essay with pictures, maps and diagrams. Try to show how cars affect your life and your town.

---- optional activity ----

4 Look at the song.

a What do you think the missing words are?

b Listen and check your ideas.

Born to be wild

Get your .... running.
Head out on the ....
Looking for ....
In whatever .... our way.

Yeh, darling, go and .... it happen.
Take the .... in a love embrace.
Fire all of your .... at once and
Explode into ....

Like a streak of ....
Heavy metal ....
Racing with the ....
And the .... that I'm under.

Yeh, darling, ... and make it happen.
Take the world in a love embrace.
Fire all of your guns at once and
Explode into space.

Like a true nature's ....
We were born, ... to be wild.
We can .... so high.
I never want to ....
Born .... be wild.
Born to .... wild.

Learning diary 5

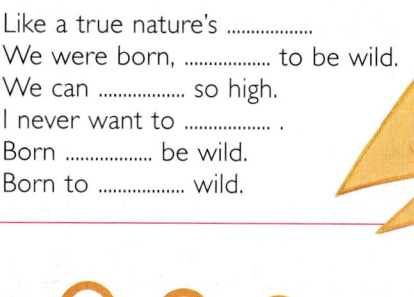

What have you learnt in this unit?

A Do the self-check in the Workbook.

B Look back at the reading texts on page 48. Find one example of each of these parts of speech.

verb   preposition
noun   pronoun
adjective   article
adverb   conjunction

Complete your Learning diary.

▶ Pronunciation: page 111

6 faraway places

Learning objectives

Learning preview: Learning a foreign language

Victoria Road: Going for a day out

Language work: Question tags ▶ 6.1–2
want someone to… ▶ 6.3

Listening: Large numbers ▶ 6.4
'if' clauses (2) ▶ 6.5

Interaction: Making and justifying choices

Reading: Describing a country
Percentages and fractions ▶ 6.4

Guided writing: Showing contrast: 'but', 'however', 'although'

Learning preview: *Learning a foreign language*

1 Read this letter to the English learners' Problem Page.

> *Dear Problem Page*
>
> *Why is learning a foreign language so difficult? There are all the words to learn and English grammar is so complicated. Some of the rules are very strange, like making questions with 'don't' and 'doesn't'. Then there are always irregular forms and exceptions. I make so many mistakes. Why can't English grammar be nice and simple like my own language? I didn't have any problems learning that.*

2 In your group, discuss the letter.

- Why do you think the grammar of the writer's own language seems easier than English grammar?
- Think about your language. Does it have any complicated structures or irregular forms?
- Why do we find learning our mother tongue easier than learning a foreign language?

3 Make a class list of ways in which you can make learning English more like learning your own language.

The picnic

1 What do you remember? What happened in the last part of the story? Look back at pages 42 and 43. Check your ideas.

2 Put these sentences in the correct order to match the picture story.

- A Kim finds Andrea and Vince on the ground together.
- B Kim drives away.
- C They stop for a picnic.
- D Kim goes back to the car to get some tissues.
- E Vince starts sneezing.
- F Terry, Vince and Andrea have to walk home.
- G Vince and Kim have an argument.
- H Kim, Vince, Terry and Andrea go out for the day.
- I Andrea tries to help Vince.
- J Vince falls over.

3 Listen and follow in your book.

Terry It must be nice to have your own wheels, Kim.

Kim You like travelling, don't you, Terry?

Terry Yes, give me the wide, open spaces. That's what I really liked about Oz. It's such a big country.

Vince You've got relations in Australia, haven't you, Andrea?

Andrea Oh, I see. Oz is Australia. Yes, that's right. My brother and his wife live in Sydney.

Later

Kim Mmm. It's nice and quiet here, isn't it?

Vince Atishoo!

Kim Bless you!

Terry You aren't getting a cold, are you? You've got to be OK for the gig next weekend.

Vince It's all right. I think it's only hay fever.

Terry Right. Well, I'll go and look for a good spot for the picnic.

Vince Atishoo! Atishoo!

Kim Look. I've got some tissues in the car. I'll just go and get them for you.

Vince Do you want me to go?

Kim No, it's all right, thanks. I'll go. I want to get my jumper anyway.

VICTORIA ROAD

Having fun?

Let's move over there till Terry gets back. Come on. ... Aargh!

Oh, Vince. Are you all right? Let me help you.

I don't want you to say anything, Vince. I just want you to leave me alone.

But you can't leave us here. How will we get home with all this gear?

This reminds me of when I was in Australia. Well, it was really hot, we were miles from anywhere and ...

Oh, shut up, Terry.

While Kim is at the car

Andrea This place isn't very sunny, is it?

Vince No, and there are lots of ants around. We don't want them to eat our food – or us, do we? Let's move over there till Terry gets back. Come on. ... Aargh!

Andrea Oh, Vince. Are you all right? Let me help you.

Kim Having fun?

A few minutes later

Vince Look. I've already explained. It wasn't what you thought. I'd fallen over and Andrea was helping me. What more do you want me to say?

Kim I don't want you to say anything, Vince. I just want you to leave me alone.

Vince But you can't leave us here. How will we get home with all this gear?

Kim That's your problem, isn't it?

Kim drives away

Terry Kim isn't leaving, is she?

Vince What does it look like? Well, we might as well have some lunch. Then I suppose we'd better try to hitch a lift home.

Later

Terry This reminds me of when I was in Australia. Well, it was really hot, we were miles from anywhere and ...

Vince Oh, shut up, Terry.

What do you think?

- Why does Kim get angry?
- What will happen now between Kim and Vince?
- What will happen about the gig?

4 Answer these questions.

a Why did Terry like Australia?
b Where does Andrea's brother live?
c What does Terry do when they stop?
d Why doesn't Vince go to fetch the tissues?
e Why do Andrea and Vince decide to move?
f What happens?
g How do they all get home?

Useful expressions

5 How do you say these expressions in your language?

It must be nice (great) to …

Having fun?

Bless you!

That's your problem.

What does it look like?

We might as well …

to hitch a lift

--- optional activities ---

LANGUAGE USE

6 Find examples in the story of people doing the things below.

- offering to help
- making suggestions

What do they actually say?

7
a 🔊 Close your book. Listen again.

b Work in groups of four. Each person takes one of the roles. Read the dialogue.

FOLLOW UP

8 Terry is telling Rosy about the day out. Copy and complete his story.

We stopped somewhere .... the country. I went to look .... a good .... for the picnic. Kim went .... to the car to get some .... because Vince was sneezing. She wanted her .... , too. Well, Vince .... to move the picnic gear, because it wasn't very .... where they were and there were a lot of .... But while he was moving the stuff, he fell .... Andrea was helping .... and just at that moment, Kim .... back. Kim and Vince had a big .... Kim drove off and .... us there.

LANGUAGE WORK

Question tags ▶ 6.1–2

1 Copy and complete these two sentences from the story on pages 52 and 53.

It's nice and quiet here, ... ?

You aren't getting a cold, ... ?

a The part that you have just completed is called a question tag. What effect does it have?

b A statement with a question tag is less direct than a normal question. We usually use a question tag when we are fairly sure of the answer. Here are some rules for making question tags. Find examples in the story to illustrate each rule.

---

1 **When the statement is positive, the tag is negative.**
Example
_____

When the statement is negative, the tag is positive.
Example
_____

2 **With the verb 'to be', we form the tag with the verb and the subject.**
Example
_____

3 **When the verb has an auxiliary, we form the tag with the auxiliary and the subject.**
Example
_____

4 **When the verb hasn't got an auxiliary, we form the tag with the auxiliary that we would normally use for making questions with that tense.**
Example
_____

5 **When the subject of the statement is a noun, we change the noun to a pronoun in the tag.**
Example
_____

---

c Translate your examples. Compare English question tags with your own language.

2 Complete these dialogues. Put the question tags on the sentences.

a
You haven't seen my song book, ...?
No. You lent it to Terry, ...?
Oh yes, so I did.

b
Terry Moore lives next door to you, ...?
Yes, that's right.
He isn't still away, ...?
No, he's been back a few weeks now.

c
We'll have to get the six o'clock train, ...?
Yes, and you won't forget the tickets, ...?
Oh, thanks for reminding me.

want someone to ... ▶ 6.3

3 Look at these sentences from the Victoria Road story on pages 52 and 53.

Do you want .... go?

We don't want .... our food.

I don't want .... anything, Vince.

I just want .... me alone.

a Copy and complete them.

b Translate the sentences into your own language.

4 What do these people want?

Example
Rosy wants Terry to help with the speakers.

Rosy: Can you help me with these speakers, Terry?

Kim: Can you check my brakes, please, Mr Scott?

Andrea: Can you explain what an M.O.T. is, please, Kim?

Mrs Moore: Can you go to the shops for me, Terry?

5 What do these people not want? What do they want instead?

Example
Rosy doesn't want Terry to put his drink on the amp. She wants him to put it on the floor.

Rosy: Don't put your drink on the amp, Terry. Put it on the floor.

Mrs Scott: Don't play your music so loud, Vince. Put your headphones on.

Mrs Moore: Don't telephone me, Vince. Just leave me alone.

Kim: You shouldn't get a job, Terry. You should get some more qualifications.

— optional activity —

FOLLOW UP

6 Write your answers to Exercises 4 and 5.

LISTENING

Journey to the stars

1 Read the text and answer the questions.

a What will people do in the next century?
b What is important about Barnard's Star?
c How far away is it?
d What is a light year?

> In the next century people will travel to other planets in our solar system. But could we ever travel to the stars? I believe that we could, but the problems would be enormous. The biggest problem would be distance. The nearest star that has planets is called Barnard's Star. It's six light years away from the Earth. That means it takes six years for light to travel from Barnard's Star to Earth.

2 You will hear a scientist talking about travelling to the planets around Barnard's Star.

a First listen and repeat these numbers.

5,000,000	750	250,000
1,000,000	40,000	900,000,000
84	100	130,000,000
10,800	22,600	

b Discuss these questions. Choose from the numbers above.

1 How long do you think it would take to reach Barnard's Star, if you travelled at 1 million kilometres an hour (km/h)?
2 How fast can our fastest rocket travel?
3 How fast could the Apollo moon rockets travel?
4 How fast would a rocket have to travel to reach Barnard's Star in a human lifetime?

c Listen and check your ideas.

3 The scientist mentions four spaceships or rockets.

a Copy the chart below.
b Listen and write their names in your chart.

spaceship	speed	time to reach Barnard's Star

c Listen again. Complete as much of the second two columns as you can.
d Calculate the missing times and complete your chart.

Large numbers ▶ 6.4

4 a Say these.

2,500,000   49,300   1,000
670,000   785,000,000

b Write these in figures.

seven hundred and twenty million
eight million, nine hundred thousand
one hundred and fifty thousand
ninety million, six hundred and ten thousand

'if' clauses (2) ▶ 6.5

5 **Complete this sentence.**

If Spaceship X .... at one million kilometres an hour, it .... Barnard's Star in six thousand five hundred years.

a Which tense is used:
   - in the **if** clause?
   - in the main clause?

b Look at the information in your chart in Exercise 3. Write a similar sentence about each of the spaceships.

—— optional activities ——

6 **What other problems would there be in travelling to Barnard's Star?**

a What things would the astronauts need?

b Would you like to be on the spaceship? Why? Why not?

FOLLOW UP

7 **Copy and complete the text below with these verbs. Some are used more than once.**

die   be   arrive   want   not know   like
have to   return   be born   go

If we *wanted* to reach Barnard's Star in less than a human lifetime – say, fifty years – the spaceship .... travel at one hundred and thirty million kilometres an hour. But the rocket .... only one of the problems. What about the astronauts? They .... take everything in the spaceship – everything – air, water, clothes, food, trees, animals, houses, schools, hospitals, because the spaceship .... their home for most of their lives. None of these astronauts .... to Earth. Some astronauts .... on the journey, others .... in space, and they .... Earth at all. If you .... on the spaceship, you .... as old as your grandparents when you .... to be one of those astronauts?

INTERACTION

Stranded

1 **Read this information.**

You are stranded. You and two other passengers were in a small spaceship which was on its way to a space colony on the planet of Tegsal. But the spaceship has crash landed on the planet. You had all been asleep for a few hours when the crash happened, and the pilot is dead, so you have no idea where you are.

You have just walked to the top of a small hill to look around. You seem to be in a desert. There is no sign of any people for at least 100 kilometres in any direction. In the distance you can see the sea. Perhaps you're on an island?

Nobody knows where you are, so you must try to find help. First you must decide what to take with you. The other two passengers are slightly injured, so you can't carry much.

2 **The items below survived the crash.**

a box of matches	a set of maps of Tegsal
pillows	a gun and ammunition
a compass	a pair of binoculars
an umbrella	10 metres of rope
a mirror	a torch with batteries
a stretcher	an inflatable boat
20 gold coins	a pair of scissors
paper and pencils	15 litres of water
blankets	a camera and film
a Walkman radio	toothbrushes and toothpaste
sleeping bags	spare pairs of boots
a first aid kit	a box of biscuits

a Work in groups of three. Choose ten items to take with you. You can't divide any of them.

b You may have to get rid of some of the things on your journey, so you must put them in order of importance.

3 **Present and justify your choice to the class.**

—— optional activity ——

FOLLOW UP

Write down your list of ten items. Say why you would choose each one.

READING

Oz

1 What do you know about Australia?

  a Write down everything that you know about Australia.

  b Compare your ideas with a partner.

  c Read the text and check your ideas.

There are many names for Australia – Oz, Down Under, and the official name, the Commonwealth of Australia – but the name that the Australians like is 'the Lucky Country'. It probably didn't seem very lucky to the first European settlers. They were convicts who had been transported from Britain. However, after gold was discovered in the 1850s, thousands of free settlers left the cold, dark industrial towns of Britain to find their place in the sun.

Australia has a population of about sixteen and a half million people. In a country of over seven and a half million square kilometres – the sixth largest in the world – this is a very small population. At least three cities in the world have larger populations than the whole of Australia. Over half the population lives in the south-east corner of the country between the two state capitals of Sydney and Melbourne.

Over eighty per cent of Australia's inhabitants are of British origin, and this can be seen in many aspects of Australian life. English is the national language, cricket is the national game, and they drive on the left. In recent years, however, most immigrants have come from other European countries such as Italy, Greece and Poland, or from Asian countries. Only about one per cent of the inhabitants are Aborigines.

A few examples of Australian English

G'day	Hello
a tinnie	a can of beer
a Pom	someone from Britain
a barbie	a barbecue
this arvo	this afternoon
a station	a farm

① ....

Many people in Australia live hundreds of miles away from the nearest school or hospital. Children study at home and they talk to their teacher by radio. If someone is ill the Flying Doctor will visit them by plane.

② ....

Some of Australia's sheep stations are larger than some countries.

③ ....

Australia has two of the most poisonous spiders in the world – the black widow and the Sydney funnel web. All children learn first aid for spider bites at school.

④ ....

⑤ ....

Australia is a huge country and has a wide range of climates from the tropical rain forest of the Northern Territory and northern Queensland to the mild temperate climate of Victoria and Tasmania in the south east. About two-thirds of the land is desert or semi-desert.

Although Sydney, with its beautiful harbour, bridge and opera house, is the largest city, it isn't the capital. Australia is a federal state and, like the United States of America, it has a separate capital city – Canberra – which isn't in any of the states themselves. The Commonwealth of Australia consists of six states (Western Australia, Queensland, South Australia, New South Wales, Victoria and Tasmania) and two territories (the Northern Territory and the Canberra Capital Territory). The Head of Government is the Prime Minister, but the Head of State is still the British monarch.

Mining, industry and agriculture are Australia's most important sources of income. More recently, tourism has become important, too. Tourists come to enjoy Australia's warm climate, to see the unique animals, such as the kangaroo, the koala and the platypus, and to see beautiful natural features like the Great Barrier Reef and the mysterious Ayers Rock.

2 Read the text again.

a Copy and complete this table.

Official name	
Area	
Population	
Language	
Currency	
Largest city	
Capital city	
Political structure	
Head of Government	
Head of State	
Main sources of income	

b Which piece of information is not in the text? Can you provide it?

3 What are the missing labels on the map?

4 Find these things in the text.

a four things that show the British origins of the population
b four types of climate that Australia has
c three things that tourists might see in Sydney
d three things that they might see outside Sydney

Percentages and fractions

▶ 6.4

5 a Find these numbers in the text.

1/2   7.5 million   80%   2/3

b Copy and complete the table. Say the numbers.

percentage	fraction
80%	/5
	1/3
30%	/10
25%	
	3/4

c Copy and complete these sentences from the text.

Over .... Australia's inhabitants are of British origin.

About .... the land is desert or semi-desert.

Over .... the population lives in the south-east corner.

d What do you notice about 'half'?

---- optional activities ----

6 Discussion points

a What do you think is the most interesting piece of information about Australia on these pages?

b Why do you think Australia is called 'the Lucky Country'?

FOLLOW UP

7 Look at the text and the picture again. What information do they give about these things? Write one or two sentences about each one.

a The Flying Doctor   c Canberra
b Animals   d Sydney

GUIDED WRITING

Showing contrast: 'but', 'however', 'although'

1 Look at these two sentences.

Sydney is the largest city. It isn't the capital.

a There is a contrast between these two sentences, because we would normally expect the largest city to be the capital. We can show this contrast in three ways.

Sydney is the largest city, <u>but</u> it isn't the capital.
Sydney is the largest city. <u>However</u>, it isn't the capital.
<u>Although</u> Sydney is the largest city, it isn't the capital.

b In what way is 'however' different from the other two? How many sentences are there?

c Find more examples of 'but', 'however' and 'although' in the text on pages 58–9.

d What do you notice about the position of 'however'?

2 Join these sentences with 'but', 'however' and 'although'.

a Australia is the sixth largest country in the world. It has a small population.
b Australia is a huge country. Over two-thirds of the land is desert.
c Most of the people are of British origin. Most recent immigrants have come from Asia.
d Most people call the country Australia. Its official name is the Commonwealth of Australia.
e Canberra is the capital. Sydney is the largest city.

Your country

3 Imagine that some English-speaking visitors are coming to your town. You want to give them a brief introduction to your country or region.

Here are some things that you could provide information about.

- the population
- the political structure
- the climate
- industries
- land use (farms, forests, etc.)
- things that the area is famous for
- animals and plants that visitors might see
- some interesting places that they could visit

▶ Pronunciation: page 111

— optional activity —

Project suggestion

4 Illustrate your text with maps and pictures. You can present your project as a poster or as a brochure.

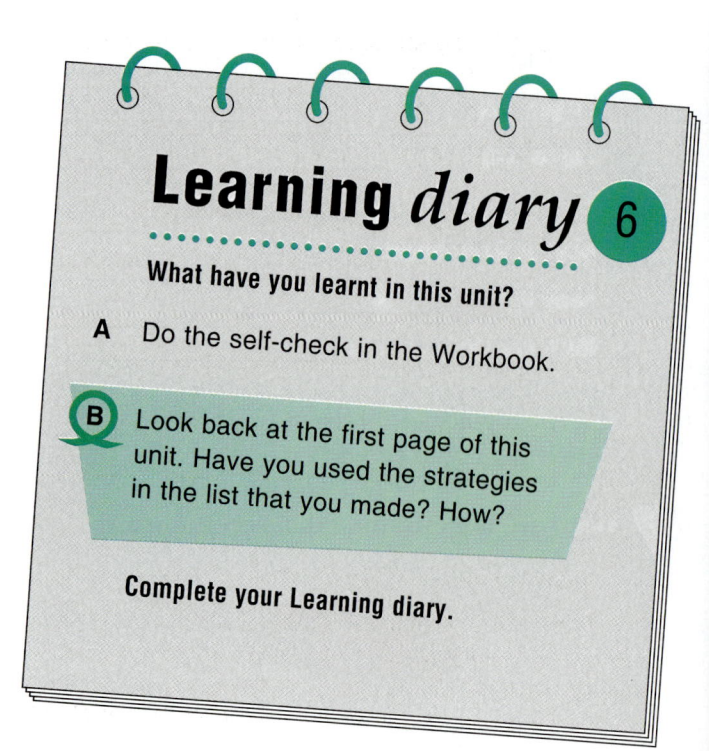

Learning *diary* 6

What have you learnt in this unit?

A Do the self-check in the Workbook.

B Look back at the first page of this unit. Have you used the strategies in the list that you made? How?

Complete your Learning diary.

7 conflict

Learning objectives

Learning preview: Group work

Victoria Road: Describing a problem
Reporting a conversation ▶ 7.1–3

Language work: Reported speech statements and questions ▶ 7.1–3

Listening: Talking about films
Descriptive vocabulary

Interaction: Agreeing and disagreeing ▶ 7.6

Reading: A story
Indirect commands and requests ▶ 7.4

Guided writing: Reference

Learning preview: *Group work*

In language learning, you often work in groups. How do you feel about group work?

a Read these statements. Which ones do you agree with?

1 It's a chance to share knowledge and information.

2 It's a chance to have a rest because the teacher isn't looking all the time.

3 It gives more variety to the lesson.

4 I do all the work and the others do nothing.

5 I could do much more on my own.

6 You can learn a lot from other students.

7 We waste a lot of time getting into groups.

8 We can do much more interesting things in groups – role plays, games and projects.

9 It's OK. It depends who I'm with.

10 We have to work much harder in groups because we all have to do something.

b Discuss your ideas with other members of the class.

A bit of a problem

1 What do you remember? What happened in the last part of the story? Look back at pages 52 and 53. Check your ideas.

2 Look at the pictures. Say whether these statements are right or wrong.

a Rosy and Dan go to see Kim at the hairdresser's.
b Kim isn't going to sing at the dance.
c She's going away to stay with a friend.
d Rosy, Vince and Dan are at Vince's house.
e Vince goes to see Kim.
f Rosy and Dan are annoyed.
g Andrea wants Vince to help her with her homework.
h Dan thinks that Andrea can help the band.

Kim No, I'm not. I wouldn't be able to sing properly after what's happened. Vince used to sing with the band. Let him do it. Anyway, I'm going away and I won't be back till Monday.

Rosy Oh, Kim! Where are you going?

Kim I'm going to see my grandad. He isn't very well. I'm sorry, Rosy, but I've made up my mind.

Later at Vince's house

Rosy Bad news, I'm afraid. Kim won't be there on Saturday.

Vince Oh no! What did she say?

Rosy She said that she had seen you with Andrea. You had been lying on the ground with her and …

Dan Forget about Casanova here. What about the gig? Did you ask her about that?

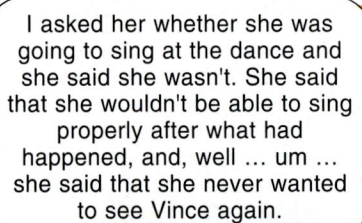

Picture 1:
— Are you going to sing at the dance?
— No, I'm not. I wouldn't be able to sing properly after what's happened. Vince used to sing with the band. Let him do it. Anyway, I'm going away and I won't be back till Monday.
— Oh, Kim! Where are you going?
— I'm going to see my grandad. He isn't very well. I'm sorry, Rosy, but I've made up my mind.

Picture 2:
— I asked her whether she was going to sing at the dance and she said she wasn't. She said that she wouldn't be able to sing properly after what had happened, and, well … um … she said that she never wanted to see Vince again.
— Well, nor do I after the trouble his love life has caused, but I'm not going to sulk about it.

Picture 3:
— I'll go and talk to Kim.
— It's too late for that. She said she was going away and she wouldn't be back till Monday. I asked her where she was going and she … well, she … she said that she was going to see her grandad, because he wasn't very well.

3 Listen and follow in your book.

Kim How would you feel, Rosy? I saw him with Andrea. He was lying on the ground with her. And he obviously doesn't care about me, because he hasn't been in touch with me since the picnic! I never want to see Vince Scott again.

Rosy But what about Saturday? Are you going to sing at the dance?

VICTORIA ROAD

Rosy Of course I did. I asked her whether she was going to sing at the dance and she said she wasn't. She said that she wouldn't be able to sing properly after what had happened, and, well … um …, she said that she never wanted to see Vince again.

Dan Well, nor do I after the trouble his love life has caused, but I'm not going to sulk about it.

Vince I'll go and talk to Kim.

Rosy It's too late for that. She said she was going away and she wouldn't be back till Monday. I asked her where she was going and she … well, she … she said that she was going to see her grandad, because he wasn't very well. She said that she was sorry but she'd made up her mind. She said you could do the singing, Vince.

Vince What? I can't sing with this cold.

Dan Oh, this is marvellous. Just wonderful. Our first big event. And what happens? Our singer's going away for the weekend. Well, I'm getting pretty annoyed about this.

Rosy So am I. Look, just calm down and sit down, Dan. And don't get at me. It isn't my fault.

Dan It isn't mine, either. I know perfectly well whose fault it is, Rosy. But what the heck are we going to do?

Andrea Vince, could you help me with this … oh, hi, Rosy, Dan. I'm sorry. You're busy. I'll come back later.

Vince Yes, OK, Andrea.

Dan No, just a minute, Andrea. Don't go. Perhaps you can help us. You see, we've got a bit of a problem.

What do you think?

- Whose fault is 'the problem'?
- Do you believe Kim's story?
- What does Dan want Andrea to do?
- What should she do?

4 Copy and complete these sentences with the correct subject.

a .... isn't going to sing at the dance on Saturday.

b .... has been to see Kim.

c .... has got a cold.

d .... is annoyed.

e .... doesn't think it's her fault.

f .... comes in while they are talking.

g .... thinks Andrea can help the band.

Useful expressions

5 How do you say these expressions in your language? Do you know any other English expressions with a similar meaning?

I've made up my mind.

Forget about...

Don't get at me.

I know perfectly well...

What the heck are we going to do?

We've got a bit of a problem.

---
optional activities

LANGUAGE USE

6 Rosy, Dan and Vince each take a different attitude towards the problem.

  a What is each person's attitude?

  b How does their attitude show in what they say and how they say it?

7 a 📼 Close your book. Listen again.

  b Work in groups of four. One person is Kim and Andrea, one is Rosy, one is Dan and one is Vince. Read the dialogue.

FOLLOW UP

8 Answer these questions.

  a Why doesn't Kim want to sing at the dance?
  b What is she going to do?
  c How does she feel about Vince?
  d Why does Rosy say 'It's too late'?
  e Why is Dan annoyed?
  f How can Andrea help the band?

LANGUAGE WORK

Reported speech: statements ▶ 7.1

1 What did Kim tell Rosy? What did Rosy tell the others?

I saw him with Andrea.
He was lying on the ground.
I never want to see Vince again.
I'm going away.
I won't be back till Monday.
I wouldn't be able to sing properly.
I've made up my mind.

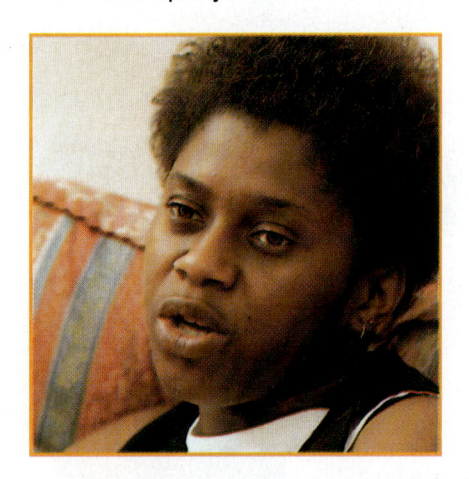

a Complete what Rosy says. Use the Victoria Road story on pages 62 and 63 to help you.

Kim said that ...

... she .... you with Andrea.

... you .... on the ground.

... she never .... to see Vince again.

... she .... away.

... she .... back till Monday.

... she .... able to sing properly.

... she .... her mind.

b How do the tenses change in reported speech? Copy and complete this table.

direct speech	indirect speech
past simple	....
past continuous	....
present simple	....
present continuous	....
future with *will*	....
conditional	....
present perfect	....

c How do the pronouns change when Rosy reports what Kim said? Why?

2 Terry wasn't with the group. Rosy is telling him what Andrea said. Look at what Andrea said. What did Rosy say to Terry?

Example
She said that Kim was being unfair.

a Kim is being unfair.
b Vince fell over.
c I don't want to upset Kim any more.
d If I take her place, Kim will be very angry.
e I've never sung on stage before.
f I'd be very nervous.
g I don't know all of the songs.

Reported speech: questions ▶ 7.3

3 Look at Rosy's two questions to Kim.

Are you going to sing at the dance?

Where are you going?

a What did Rosy say to Vince and Dan?

b Look at your sentences in **a**. Copy and complete these rules. Use these words.

subject **whether** verb question word

> In 'Yes/No' questions the word order for reported questions is:
> reporting verb + _____ + _____ + _____ .

> In 'Wh-' questions the word order for reported questions is:
> reporting verb + _____ + _____ + _____ .

c Translate the sentences in **a**. Compare the rules for making reported questions in your language with the English rules in **b**.

4 Here are some more questions that Rosy asked Kim. How would she report these to Dan and Vince?

Example
I asked her what Vince had done.

a What did Vince do?
b Have you spoken to Vince since the picnic?
c Why are you going away?
d What will you do?
e Are you going on your own?
f Can I do anything to help?
g How can the band perform without a singer?

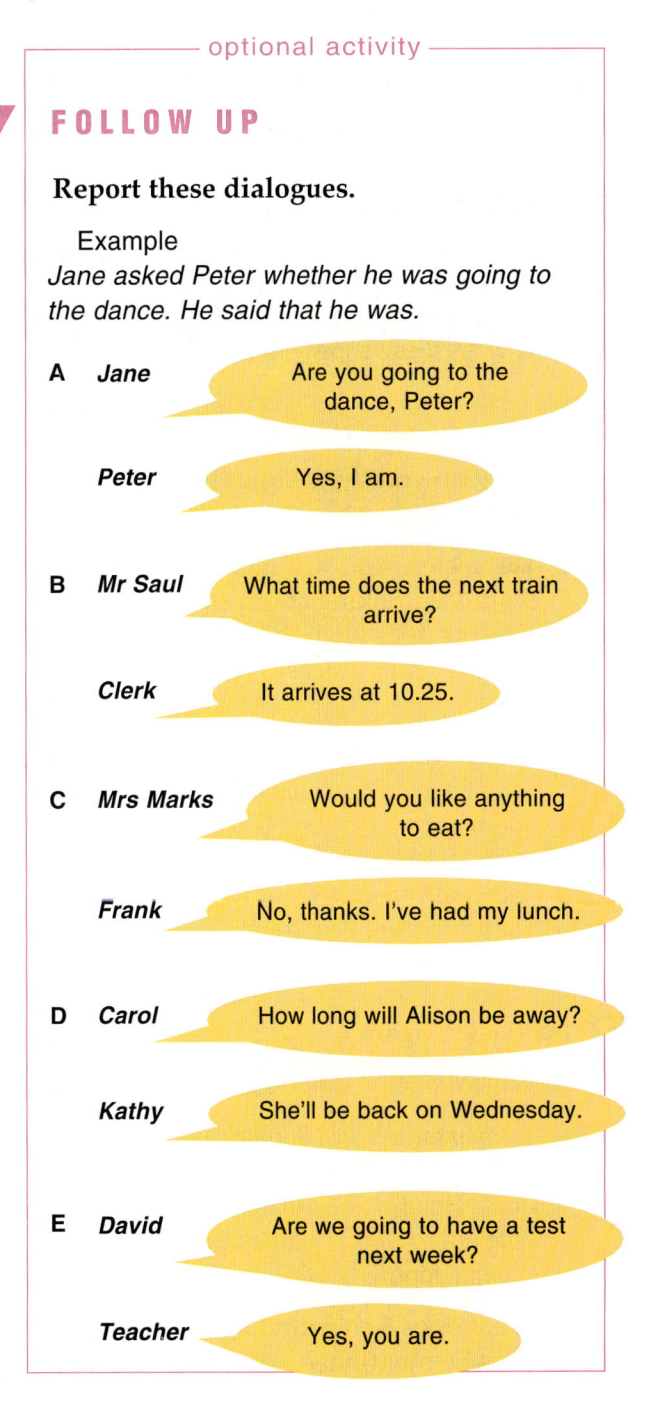

— optional activity —

5 FOLLOW UP

Report these dialogues.

Example
Jane asked Peter whether he was going to the dance. He said that he was.

A Jane: Are you going to the dance, Peter?
 Peter: Yes, I am.

B Mr Saul: What time does the next train arrive?
 Clerk: It arrives at 10.25.

C Mrs Marks: Would you like anything to eat?
 Frank: No, thanks. I've had my lunch.

D Carol: How long will Alison be away?
 Kathy: She'll be back on Wednesday.

E David: Are we going to have a test next week?
 Teacher: Yes, you are.

LISTENING

Superheroes, super profits

1 Read the text below.

> Films with comic book heroes like Batman or real-life heroes like James Bond are big business. Why are these superhero films so popular?

a What superhero films have you seen?

b Why do you think superhero films are popular?

c 📼 Listen. You will hear a film critic, Ken Saunders, talking about the films. What reasons does he give for their popularity? Choose from this list.

They are cheap to make.
They have amazing special effects.
They have complicated stories.
The heroes are big stars like Arnold Schwarzenegger.
They are very violent.
The stories are very simple.
The whole family can enjoy them.

2 📼 Listen again.

a Which of these does Ken Saunders mention?

Terminator II	Superman
Star Wars	The Empire Strikes Back
Robin Hood	Raiders of the Lost Ark
Batman	James Bond
Indiana Jones	George Lucas

b What does Ken Saunders say about the ones he mentions?

---

optional activities

WORD WORK

3 What does Ken describe with these adjectives?

spectacular	complicated	incredible
amazing	simple	exciting
good	bad	rough and tough
huge	high	gentle

4 Discussion points

a What features should these characters have: the ideal hero; the ideal heroine; the ideal villain?

b Why do you think the films discussed are only about heroes and not heroines? What would a 'superheroine' film be like?

FOLLOW UP

5 Write a summary of what Ken Saunders says and add your own opinion. Follow this pattern.

*Ken Saunders thinks that there are two reasons why superhero films are popular.
The first reason is that ... . For example, ...
The second reason is that ... . The story is always ... . Life is not really like this, but people don't go ... . They go ...
The ideal superhero is ... and ...
I like/don't like these films, because ...*

INTERACTION

Agreeing and disagreeing

▶ 7.6

1 Look at these extracts from the Victoria Road story on pages 62 and 63.

Rosy She said that she never wanted to see Vince again.
Dan Well, ...

Dan Well, I'm getting pretty annoyed about this.
Rosy ....

a Copy them and complete the replies.

b Look at the story to check your answers.

c Copy and complete these rules.

> To agree with a positive statement we use
> _____ + auxiliary + subject.
> Examples
> 'I come from Australia.' | 'I can play the guitar.'
> 'So do I.' | 'So can I.'

> To agree with a negative statement we use
> _____ + auxiliary + subject.
> Examples
> 'I'm not from London.' | 'I haven't seen that film.'
> 'Nor am I.' | 'Nor have I.'

2 🔊 Listen. The speaker will make some statements. Agree with what the speaker says. Then repeat the correct response. It's a 'rap', so try to keep the rhythm.

Example
Speaker 1 I like diving.
You So do I.
Speaker 2 So do I.
You So do I.

3 Here are the rules for disagreeing.

a To disagree with a positive statement we usually say **Oh, I** + *negative* auxiliary.

Examples
'I like curry.' | 'I can play the guitar.'
'Oh, I don't.' | 'Oh, I can't.'

b To disagree with a negative statement we usually say Oh, I + positive auxiliary.

Examples
'I'm not tired.' | 'I haven't finished.'
'Oh, I am.' | 'Oh, I have.'

4 Listen again. This time, disagree.

Example
Speaker 1 I like diving.
You Oh, I don't.
Speaker 2 Oh, I don't.
You Oh, I don't.

5 Look at this questionnaire.

Question	Me	My partner
1 Do you sleepwalk?		
2 Have you got a pet?		
3 Would you like to be a pop star?		
4 Are you good at sport?		
5 Do you ever help with housework?		
6 Can you usually remember your dreams?		
7 Have you ever seen a ghost?		
8 Did you answer these questions honestly?		

a Answer the questions by writing **Yes** or **No**. Don't show your answers to anyone.

b Work with a partner. Student A gives his/her answer. Student B agrees or disagrees. Note down each other's answer (Yes or No) in the second column.

Example
A *I don't sleepwalk.* **B** *Nor do I.* or *Oh, I do.*

c Change partners and repeat.

───── optional activity ─────

FOLLOW UP

6 Write your dialogues from Exercise 5b.

READING

The Cheetah's Eyes

1 Look at the pictures.

a Who are the main characters?

b Look quickly through the texts and find their names.

c What is happening in each picture?

2 Read the texts below.

a Number them in the correct order to match the pictures.

b Explain how you put the texts in the correct order.

A Isabel, Digby and his assistant, Moustapha, travelled into the desert. But Sir Walter's evil brother, Spencer, had also found out about the Cheetah's Eyes. He sent his men after the little group and he told them not to come back without the jewels.

B One of the barrels landed on the road in front of the car. The driver swerved to avoid the barrel and the car turned over. Digby told Moustapha to head for the airfield that was near the town.

C One day, however, King Abendula's palace was attacked. The king was killed, but one of his servants escaped with the emeralds to Egypt. Unfortunately, the servant soon died. The secret chamber and its treasure were lost, but the legend of the Cheetah's Eyes was not forgotten.

D At the airfield, a small plane was standing near the runway. Isabel and Moustapha ran towards the plane. Digby told them to start the engines.

E Long ago in the heart of Africa there lived a king called Abendula. King Abendula was fabulously rich. He kept his treasure in a secret chamber. It was full of diamonds, emeralds, sapphires, rubies and gold. The entrance to the chamber was guarded by a statue of a cheetah and the chamber could only be opened when two enormous emeralds were placed in the cheetah's eyes.

F The plane's engines roared into life, as Digby was running to the steps, but then he stopped. In the doorway of the plane was Spencer Crawford. He was holding Isabel and he had a gun. Digby told Spencer to let her go. But Spencer told him not to be silly. He said that he had got the emeralds now and there was nothing that Digby could do about it.

G Digby jumped onto the back of the lorry and Moustapha drove out of the town. Spencer's men were soon following them in their own car. In the back of the lorry there were some barrels. Digby asked Isabel to help him push the barrels off.

3 Read the texts again and answer these questions.

  a What was in King Abendula's secret chamber?
  b Why were the emeralds important?
  c Why was the secret chamber lost?
  d Where did Sir Walter find the emeralds?
  e How had they got there?
  f Why didn't Sir Walter go on the expedition?

Indirect commands and requests ▶ 7.4

4 Look at the sentences in the speech bubbles.

  a In the story these are given in reported speech. Find the reported forms.
  b Copy and complete these rules.

> **To report positive commands and requests, we use: 'asked'/'told' + person + _____ + infinitive.**

> **To report negative commands and requests, we use: 'asked'/'told' + person + _____ _____ + infinitive.**

  c When the person is shown by a pronoun, we must use an object pronoun. Find examples in the texts.

5 Here are some things that Sir Walter Crawford told Digby to do. Report what he said.

  a Buy some guns.
  b Don't lose the emeralds.
  c Look after Isabel.
  d Don't take any risks.
  e Don't tell Spencer about the treasure.

—————— optional activity ——————

FOLLOW UP

6 The story is told mostly in reported speech. What did the people actually say?

  Example
  Digby told them to start the engines.
  'Start the engines.'

  a Find more sentences in reported speech and write what the people actually said.
  b Decide how the story ends. Write the dialogue for the ending.
  c Put together your dialogues from **a** and **b** to make a play.

H But before they could start, Sir Walter became very ill. His daughter Isabel asked him not to go on the expedition. She said that she would find the treasure. Sir Walter gave the emeralds to his daughter and wished her luck.

I Many centuries later in 1946 an archaeologist called Sir Walter Crawford discovered the emeralds in a shop in Cairo. Sir Walter asked his friend Digby Maxwell to help him find the treasure.

J When Isabel, Digby and Moustapha stopped in a small town on the edge of the desert, Spencer's men attacked them. While Digby fought the men off, Isabel and Moustapha jumped into a lorry and Moustapha started the engine. Isabel shouted to Digby and told him to get on the lorry.

GUIDED WRITING

Reference

▼1 **When we write a text we can use reference to avoid repeating words and expressions.**

a Look at this paragraph. What do the underlined words refer to?

> Isabel, Digby and <u>his</u> assistant, Moustapha, travelled into the desert. But Sir Walter's evil brother, Spencer, had also found out about the Cheetah's Eyes. <u>He</u> sent <u>his</u> men after the little group and <u>he</u> told <u>them</u> not to come back without the jewels.

b The underlined words are pronouns or possessive adjectives. Find more examples of these in the story on pages 68–9. What do they refer to?

c We don't always use pronouns and possessive adjectives for reference. Sometimes we can use a different word or expression with the same meaning. Look at the paragraph in **a** again. What do these refer to?

- the little group
- the jewels

▼2 **In this text replace the underlined words with these items. Some are used more than once.**

they   the young man   Sir Walter's evil brother
his   it   his assistant   them   the old vehicle

> Spencer threw Moustapha out of the plane. Digby helped <u>Moustapha</u> to his feet, as <u>Spencer</u> closed the door. Digby and Moustapha ran to the lorry. <u>Digby and Moustapha</u> jumped in and drove <u>the lorry</u> towards the runway. <u>Digby and Moustapha</u> reached <u>the runway</u> just as the plane roared past <u>Digby and Moustapha</u>. While <u>Moustapha</u> drove the lorry, Digby fired <u>Digby's</u> gun at the plane's engines.

Film review

▼3 **Describe a film that you have seen recently.**

- Describe the main characters (job, physical appearance, personality, etc.).
- Give a brief summary of the story.
- Describe any special effects or stunts.
- Say whether you liked the film and explain why or why not.

▶ **Pronunciation: page 112**

---

optional activity

Project suggestion

▼4 Make a project about the movies.

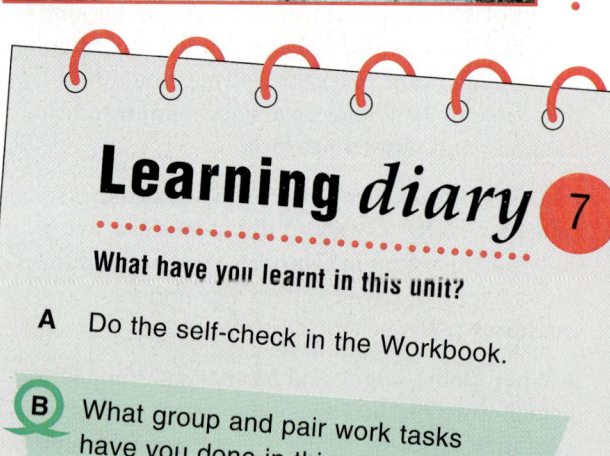

Learning *diary* 7

What have you learnt in this unit?

A   Do the self-check in the Workbook.

B   What group and pair work tasks have you done in this unit? Did you enjoy them? Were they useful?

Complete your Learning diary.

revision 8

1
**reading skills
reported questions
question tags
passive voice**

▼ 1 Who was the girl on the motorbike? Read the story quickly and find out.

▼ 2 Read the story again and find the answers to these questions.

a What time of day did the incident happen?
b Where is Wrotham Hill?
c Where was the girl when Clive first saw her?
d Why was he surprised to see her?
e What happened at the phone box?
f What was surprising about the policeman's attitude?
g In what year had the accident happened?

The girl on the motorbike

In the early hours of 5 April 1989 a motorbike was speeding along the A20 in Kent.

As he approached Wrotham Hill, Clive Taylor looked at his watch. Exactly two o'clock. Five minutes later he reached the bend at the top of the hill. It was a dangerous place for accidents.

Suddenly, he saw a girl. She was standing in the middle of the road. Clive had to swerve to avoid her, but she didn't move. When he had stopped, the girl calmly walked up to him and asked him if he could give her a lift. He asked her what she was doing there. She said that there had been an accident. Clive looked around, but he couldn't see a car or any other people.

Clive told the girl to get on the pillion and to hold tight. As she climbed on, Clive suddenly felt very cold, but he noticed that she was only wearing a light dress. She looked as if she was on her way to a party.

At the bottom of the hill there was a telephone box. Clive pulled off the road and stopped. But when he turned round, he froze in horror. The girl wasn't there.

Had she fallen off the pillion? In a cold sweat, he rode back up to the place where he had first seen the girl. But he couldn't see her. He rode down the hill again as slowly as he could. There was no sign of her. She had simply disappeared.

Clive rode to the nearest police station. He told the policeman at the desk what had happened, but to his surprise, the policeman didn't seem very worried. Then he told Clive that ten years before, there had been an accident on Wrotham Hill. A girl and her boyfriend had been on their way back from a party, when she had fallen off the pillion of the motorbike and been killed. Since that time several motorcyclists had seen the girl. The accident had happened at exactly five past two.

3 ─ optional activity ─

There are several clues in the story that there was something strange about the girl. What are the clues?

Example
She was standing in the middle of the road.

4 As they were going down the hill, Clive asked the girl some questions, but she didn't reply. Report what he asked her.

Example
He asked her what her name was.

a What's your name?
b Where do you live?
c Do you feel cold?
d Are you on your way to a party?
e How did the accident happen?
f Was anyone injured?

5 Clive is at the police station. Here are some more things that the policeman said to him. Complete them with question tags.

a You aren't from this area, ...?
b The girl was wearing a party dress, ...?
c You first saw her just after two o'clock, ...?
d It's been a bit of a shock for you, ...?
e When you went to the telephone box, the girl wasn't on the pillion, ...?
f You won't forget this easily, ...?
g You'd like a cup of tea, ...?

6 Put these sentences into the passive voice. Keep the same tense.

a The experience frightened Clive.
b A local newspaper published Clive's story.
c The newspaper received a lot of letters.
d Several other people had seen the ghost.
e A TV company will interview Clive.

─ optional activity ─

7 Make the dialogue for the story. Act your dialogue.

2 listening skills
reported speech
using a dictionary

Joey

1 Look at these pictures.

a Find these things in the pictures. Use a dictionary to help you.

budgerigar (budgie)   stepladder   bird cage
decorator   wallpaper   paint   pet shop
paintbrush   cooker   kettle

b What do you think is happening?

3 **Listen again.**

a Number these bits of dialogue in the correct order to match the pictures.

b One bit of dialogue is missing. What was said?

- A Can you help me bring up some more paint from the van?
- B Clear out the room, while I fetch the equipment from the van.
- C Have you got a blue budgie that looks the same?
- D I can smell gas.
- E I'll have a cup of tea first.
- F I'm going out.
- G Don't worry.
- H Turn off the gas.
- I We'll have to buy another budgie.

4 Here are some more things that Mrs Smith said to the two men. Report what she told or asked them to do or not to do.

a Take up all the carpets.
b Please don't make too much noise.
c Be careful with the furniture.
d Please open the windows.
e Don't leave the front door open.

5 Use the dialogue in Exercise 3. Complete the story.

Stan and Ray arrived to decorate Mrs Smith's flat. Mrs Smith told them that .... Stan told .... However, Ray thought that .... , so he went into the kitchen. As he was turning on the gas, the doorbell rang. It was Stan. He asked .... When they got back to the flat, Stan said .... They rushed into the kitchen. The room was full of gas. Ray had forgotten to light the cooker. Stan .... Then, as he was opening the window, Stan noticed a bird cage. In the bird cage was a blue budgerigar. It was dead. Stan said that .... Then he drove to the nearest pet shop. He showed the shopkeeper the dead bird and he asked .... Luckily, she did. Stan rushed back to the flat. When Mrs Smith came back, she went into the kitchen. Stan told .... When Mrs Smith came out of the kitchen she was holding the bird cage. Then she said that ....

2 Now listen and find the answers to these questions.

a What are the two men's names?
b What is the woman's name?
c Why were the two men at the flat?
d What happened in the kitchen?
e What did the men think when they saw the bird?
f Why did one of the men go to the pet shop?
g Why was the old woman pleased?

3 agreeing and disagreeing
modal + passive
(not) want someone to
second conditional
'used to'

1 Look at the dialogues. Complete them with words from the spiral. You should use all the words. Some are used more than once.

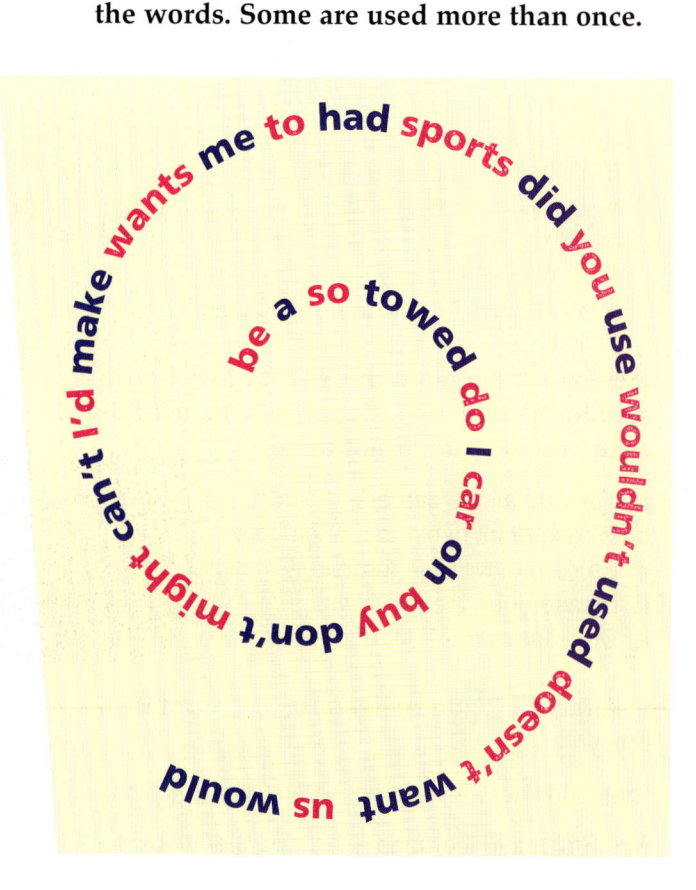

Spiral words: be a so to wed do I car oh buy don't might can't I'd make wants me to had sports did you use wouldn't used doesn't want us would

a A When I grow up, I want to be famous.
   B .... I want to be a singer.
   A .... I want to be a film star.

b C I'm sorry, but I .... it this evening.
   D Why not?
   C The boss .... to work late.

c E When you were a kid, ... watch Children's Hour?
   F Oh, yes. I .... watch it every day.

d G What's the problem?
   H The traffic warden .... park here.
   G Why not?
   H They're going to dig up the road, so it .... away.

e I If I .... lots of money, ...
   J .... I'd get a Porsche.
   I .... I'd have a Ferrari.

▶ Pronunciation: page 112

PROJECT

It's amazing

1 Look at the stories in this unit.
   a Do you believe them? Give your reasons.
   b Do you know any similar stories?

2 Look back at the Guided Writing sections in Units 1–7. What things have you learnt about?

3 Work in a group. Make a collection of amazing stories.
   a They can be funny or serious; short or long; fact or fiction; modern or traditional. You should have at least five stories.
   b Write out your stories. Stick them on a poster and illustrate them.
   c Ask people if they believe them.
   d Get other students to suggest titles for each of your stories.

MAN BITES DOG   ELVIS IS ALIVE
   QUEEN WINS LOTTERY
ALIENS STOLE MY CAR   SNOW IN THE MEDITERRANEAN IN JULY

Learning diary 8

Look back through your Learning diary.
- What have you studied so far this year?
- How well do you know these things?
- Is there anything that you still don't understand?

Check in the Grammar reference and your vocabulary notebook. Make a list of things you need to revise.

9 image

Learning objectives

Learning preview: Speaking English

Victoria Road: Having an argument

Language work: There's somebody ...ing ▶9.1
see/hear somebody ...ing ▶9.1

Listening: Talking about image and colour
Word formation, nouns and adjectives

Interaction: A conversation at the hairdresser's
'like'/'want' + present participle ▶9.1

Reading: A magazine article
'by' + present participle ▶9.1

Guided writing: Summarising

Learning preview: *Speaking English*

1 a Read this letter to the English learners' Problem Page. What is the writer's problem? Why?

> *Dear Problem Page*
>
> *I know that one of the best ways to learn a language is to use it as much as possible, but I always feel silly when I speak English. I don't like talking in front of the whole class, because I know I'm making mistakes. And I feel really silly when we have to speak English with our friends in pair or group work. I feel very self-concious, because it just isn't natural. And I know I could never speak English to English speakers, because they would laugh at my mistakes and my accent.*

b Work in groups. Discuss these questions.

- How do you feel when you speak English?
- What do you think when your friends make mistakes in English?
- Why is it important to speak English as much as possible?
- Would you laugh at someone who tried to speak your language?

c Write a reply to the letter and give the writer some advice.

2 Try to follow the advice yourself as you work through the unit.

The argument

1 What do you remember? What happened in the last part of the story? Look back at pages 62 and 63. Check your ideas.

2 Look at the picture story.

   a Where does it take place? Who is the man wearing a tie?

   b Put these sentences in the correct order to match the pictures.

   A The manager tells Vince to serve some customers.
   B Terry tells Vince about the agent.
   C Vince tells the manager to shut up.
   D Kim hides because Terry comes in.
   E Kim gets angry and runs out of the shop.
   F Vince loses his job.
   G Kim realizes that Andrea stood in for her.
   H Kim comes to talk things over with Vince.

3 Listen and follow in your book.

Vince Oh, hello, Kim. I thought I saw you looking in the window. How are you?

Kim I've had a chance to think about things and we need to talk things over, Vince. I'm very sorry about Saturday. Did you manage without me?

Vince Yes, we ... er ... we managed. Look. Can we meet for lunch? I can see Terry heading this way.

Kim Oh, no. I don't want to see him now. I'll have a look at these tracksuits till he's gone.

Terry You're gonna be a star, yeah, yeah, yeah! You're gonna be a star!

Vince What are you so excited about?

Terry You'll never guess. But you know my friend Shirley? Well, an agent she knows lives around here and he heard us playing at the dance on Saturday. He phoned me this morning and he wants to see us again.

Vince Oh, great news, Tell, but look, can we talk about it some other time? I think I can hear the telephone ringing in the back room. I ...

Terry He said we needed to change our image a bit, but ...

VICTORIA ROAD

Comic strip dialogue

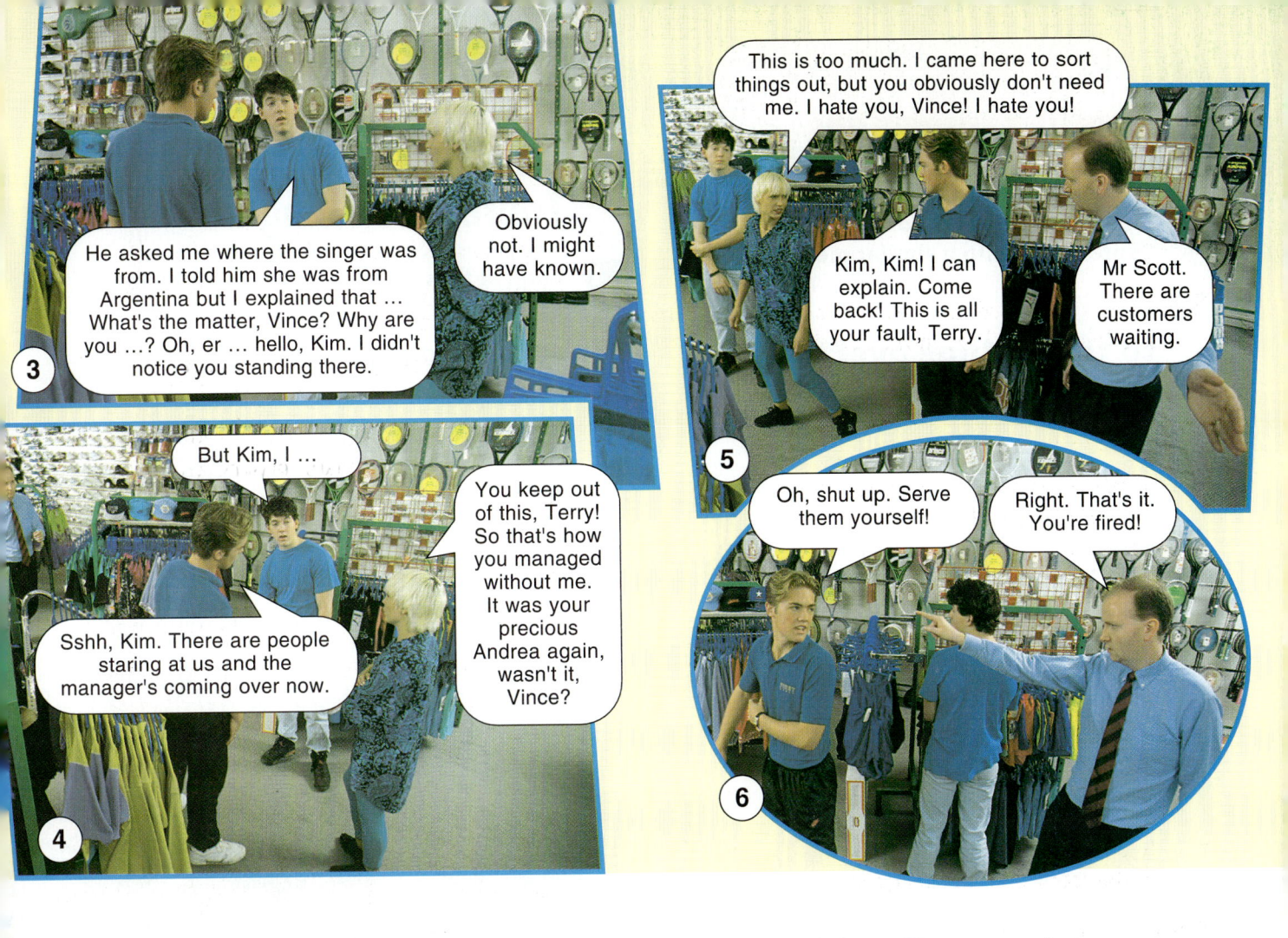

Panel 3:
- He asked me where the singer was from. I told him she was from Argentina but I explained that … What's the matter, Vince? Why are you …? Oh, er … hello, Kim. I didn't notice you standing there.
- Obviously not. I might have known.

Panel 4:
- But Kim, I …
- Sshh, Kim. There are people staring at us and the manager's coming over now.
- You keep out of this, Terry! So that's how you managed without me. It was your precious Andrea again, wasn't it, Vince?

Panel 5:
- This is too much. I came here to sort things out, but you obviously don't need me. I hate you, Vince! I hate you!
- Kim, Kim! I can explain. Come back! This is all your fault, Terry.
- Mr Scott. There are customers waiting.

Panel 6:
- Oh, shut up. Serve them yourself!
- Right. That's it. You're fired!

Vince Yes, very good. But there's someone calling me, Terry. Can we discuss it this evening?

Terry Yes, but you haven't heard the best bit yet. He asked me where the singer was from. I told him she was from Argentina but I explained that … What's the matter, Vince? Why are you …? Oh, er … hello, Kim. I didn't notice you standing there.

Kim Obviously not. I might have known.

Terry But Kim, I …

Kim You keep out of this, Terry! So that's how you managed without me. It was your precious Andrea again, wasn't it, Vince?

Vince Sshh, Kim. There are people staring at us and the manager's coming over now.

Kim I don't care. People ought to know what a rat you are, Vince Scott.

Manager Excuse me, Mr Scott. I can hear your friend shouting from the other end of the shop.

Vince Yes, I'm sorry. Just a minute. I …

Kim This is too much. I came here to sort things out, but you obviously don't need me. I hate you, Vince! I hate you!

Vince Kim, Kim! I can explain. Come back! This is all your fault, Terry.

Manager Mr Scott. There are customers waiting.

Vince Oh, shut up. Serve them yourself!

Manager Right. That's it. You're fired!

What do you think?

- What will Kim do now?
- What should Vince do?
- What will Andrea think?

Right, Wrong or Don't know?

		✓	✗	?
a	Kim is sorry about not singing at the dance.			
b	Kim hides so that Terry won't see her.	✗		
c	The agent thought that Andrea was very good.	✓		
d	Terry knows that Kim is in the shop when he comes in.		✗	
e	Kim knew that Andrea had stood in for her.	✓		
f	The manager wants Vince to serve some customers.	✓		

Useful expressions

5 How do you say these expressions in your language? Do you know any other English expressions with a similar meaning?

to talk things over

You'll never guess.

some other time

I might have known.

You keep out of this!

your precious Andrea

to sort things out

You're fired!

---

optional activities

LANGUAGE USE

6 Vince tries to avoid speaking to Kim and Terry. What excuses does he make?

7 a 📼 Close your book. Listen again.

b Work in groups of three. One person is Terry and the manager, one person is Kim and one person is Vince. Read the dialogue.

FOLLOW UP

8 Answer these questions.
a Why did Kim go to the shop?
b Why did Kim hide?
c What was Terry excited about?
d What did the agent ask Terry about Andrea?
e Why did Kim get angry?
f Why did Vince lose his job?

LANGUAGE WORK

There's sb ...ing ▶ 9.1

1 Look at these sentences from the Victoria Road story on pages 76 and 77.

A Yes, very good. But there's *someone calling* me, Terry.
B Sshh, Kim. There are *people staring* at us.
C Mr Scott. There are *customers waiting*.

a Copy and complete them.
b Translate the sentences into your own language.

2 Look at this picture. What is happening?

Examples
There's a woman parking a car.
There are three people waiting at the bus stop.

3 Are you a good witness?

a Read the instructions and close your book.

b Listen. Someone is describing the scene. Say whether the statements are right or wrong. Correct the wrong ones.

c Open your book and check your ideas.

— optional activity —

4 Look at the picture again. How many people, animals or things are there doing these things?

Example
There are ... people eating and ... people drinking.

eating or drinking	working
looking happy	doing something that they shouldn't
looking angry or worried	being friendly to someone
running	waiting
buying or selling something	sitting down

see/hear sb ...ing ▶ 9.1

5 Look at these sentences.

A I thought I saw you. You were looking in the window.
B I can hear your friend. She's shouting.

a We can express these ideas in a simpler way. Look at the Victoria Road story on pages 76 and 77. Find a shorter way of expressing the ideas.

b Find more examples of this structure in the story.

c Translate the sentences from the story into your own language.

6 Work in pairs.

a Student A chooses a person in the picture in Exercise 2. Student B describes what that person can see and hear happening.

Example
A *the girl who's running*
B *She can see the bus leaving.*

b Reverse roles and repeat.

— optional activities —

7 Pictures in your mind

a Work in pairs. Student B closes his/her eyes. Student A says a word.

b Student B describes what he/she can see or hear in his/her mind.

Example
A *thief*
B *I can see a boy running down the street. There's a man chasing him. I can hear the man shouting 'Stop'.*

FOLLOW UP

8 Choose a window in your home. Write down five things that you can see happening and five things that you can hear happening from the window.

LISTENING

Image and colour

1 What's your favourite colour? What do you associate with different colours?

2 📼 Listen. You will hear an interview with an image consultant talking about colour.

   a Look at the colours below. Which of the colours are mentioned?

   b 📼 Listen again. Connect the colours to the correct associations according to the tape.

3 Answer these questions.

   a What examples does the consultant give of groups of people who wear these colours?

      blue   red   green   white   black

   b Why do they wear them?

WORD WORK

4 Look at the list of nouns in the picture.

   a The consultant uses adjectives when she speaks. What are the adjectives for these nouns?

   b Listen again and check your ideas.

   c Some of the adjectives aren't used on the tape. Use a dictionary to find them.

---- optional activity ----

FOLLOW UP

5 Think of a product, e.g. a drink, a brand of designer clothes, sports equipment. Describe the product's image.

   a Who is the product aimed at?

   b What kind of image do the producers try to create?

   c What colours, designs or logos are used to create the image?

   d Do you think the image is successful?

---

warmth and friendliness
power and authority
excitement and danger
calmness and peace
purity and strength
relaxation
openness and freedom
anonymity

INTERACTION

At the hairdresser's

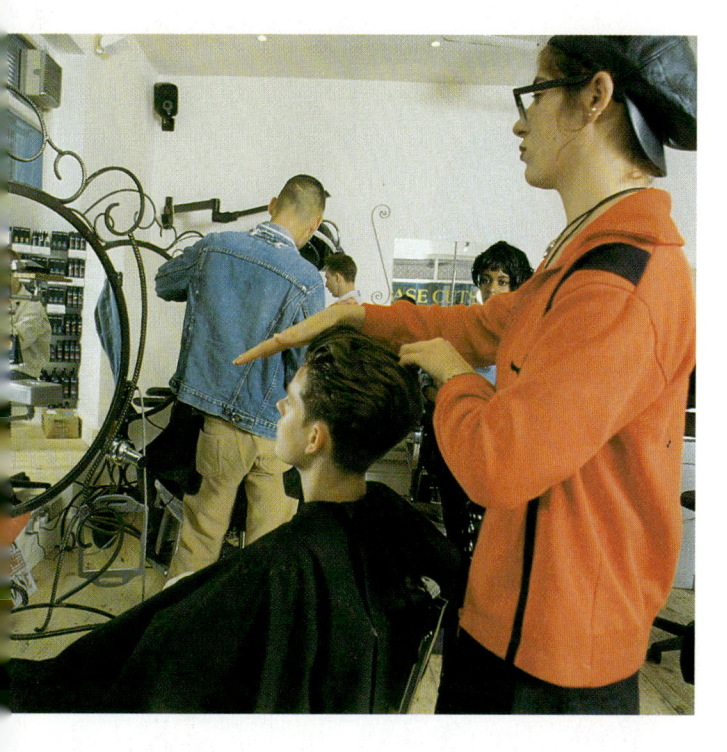

1 Look at this dialogue.

a Number the parts in the correct order.

b 📼 Listen and check your order.

A Hairdresser Fine. Now if you could just sit back over here. How much do you want taking off?

Customer About half an inch, please. And I'd like it thinning out a bit at the sides.

Hairdresser Hmm, yes. Would you like it layering?

Customer Yes, that would be good.

B Hairdresser Hello. How are you?

Customer Fine, thanks.

Hairdresser How do you want it doing?

Customer Just a trim, please.

Hairdresser Do you want it washing first?

Customer Yes, please.

C Hairdresser Well, there you are. That's £12, please.

Customer Here you are.

Hairdresser Thank you very much. Goodbye.

Customer Bye.

D Hairdresser OK, well, if you could take a seat over here. Could you just put this towel round your shoulders and then put your head back? That's it. That's not too hot, is it?

Customer No, it's fine.

Hairdresser Nice day today, isn't it?

Customer Yes, a lot better than it has been for a while.

E Hairdresser Right. Is that short enough?

Customer Yes, thanks, that's fine. I'd like some gel putting on it, please.

Hairdresser And then you want it parting at the side here and combing back. Is that right?

Customer Yes, that's it.

2 Work in pairs. Act the dialogue.

'like' / 'want' + present participle ▶ 9.1

3 Look at these sentences from the dialogue.

Do you want .... first?

Would you like .... ?

I'd like .... on it, please.

a Copy and complete them.

b Translate the sentences into your language.

4 Role play

a One person is the hairdresser and the other is the customer. Make the dialogue.

Follow this pattern for the hairdresser. The customer should respond appropriately.

Greet the customer.
Ask what he/she would like.
Ask the customer to sit down.
Ask for more details (how much to cut off/where/what colour/style).
Talk to the customer while you are working.
Ask if it is all right.
Ask if the customer wants anything else.
Give the cost and say goodbye.

b Act your dialogue.

─ optional activity ─

FOLLOW UP

5 Write your dialogue from Exercise 4.

READING

1 Look quickly at the text and the pictures.

  a What is the text about?

  b Where do you think it is from?

2 Read the text. Match the pictures to the correct paragraph.

3 Read the text again and find answers to the following questions.

  a Why do we have hair?

  b How long does an individual hair live?

  c What are the three main hair types?

  d Why is hair described as 'the most versatile part of the human body'?

4 Several groups of people are mentioned who use (or used) hairstyles as a symbol of their identity.

  a Which groups are mentioned?

  b What is (or was) their characteristic hairstyle?

WORD WORK

5 In the text find as many ways as possible of changing your hairstyle.

'by' + present participle ▶ 9.1

6 Look at the third paragraph.

  a Copy and complete these sentences.

    ... they can curl straight hair .... it.

    They can make it darker .... it.

  b Look at your list in Exercise 5. Give ten ways in which you can change your hair.

---

optional activities

7 Discussion points

  a Look at all the hairstyles in the pictures. Which do you like? Why?

  b What does your hairstyle say about you? How has it changed in your lifetime?

FOLLOW UP

8 Write your answers to Exercise 6b.

Crowning glory

1 You can cut it or let it grow long. You can decorate it with ribbons and slides. You can plait it or tie it in a bun. You can change its colour with a dye and you can change its shape with a pair of scissors. Its only real purpose is protecting your head from the sun, but it also tells other people a lot about you. There's even a musical about it. It's the most versatile part of the human body. What is it? It's hair.

2 The average human head has over 100,000 separate hair follicles and each follicle produces one hair. (Fair-haired people have more than dark-haired people, but nobody knows why.) If you didn't cut your hair, it would continue growing until it reached your knees. Each hair stops growing after about six years and falls out. Then three months later, a new hair starts growing from the follicle. We all lose between fifty and a hundred hairs a day.

3 Everyone's hair is different, but there are three basic hair types – curly, wavy and straight. But you don't have to keep the type of hair that you were born with. Hairdressers can straighten curly hair and they can curl straight hair by perming it. They can make it darker by dyeing it or lighter by bleaching it. With scissors, razors and clippers, they can create all sorts of shapes. And you needn't worry if you don't like your new style. It will always grow again.

4 If you don't want to wait for it to grow, you can wear a wig. Wigs have been worn for thousands of years. In Ancient Egypt both men and women used to shave all their hair off and wear wigs. So you can stop wondering how the Ancient Egyptians got those strange hairstyles. They were just wigs. Cleopatra was really bald!

5 Hair has always been a strong symbol of group identity. It has been used by many groups from monks to Samurai warriors. We can see the same thing today. The rasta's dreadlocks, the skinhead's stubble and the punk's spikes are all symbols of group identity.

6 Many of the things that we do with hair wouldn't be possible without a lot of equipment and cosmetics – brushes, combs, hairdryers, shampoo, conditioner, gel, mousse, grease, hairspray. Confusing, isn't it? But don't worry. In next week's issue of Teen Scene we're starting a new series on 'You and Your Hair'. It could change your whole image.

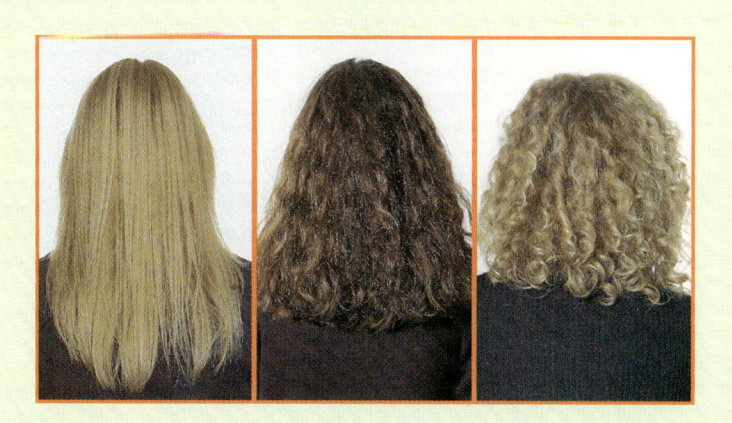

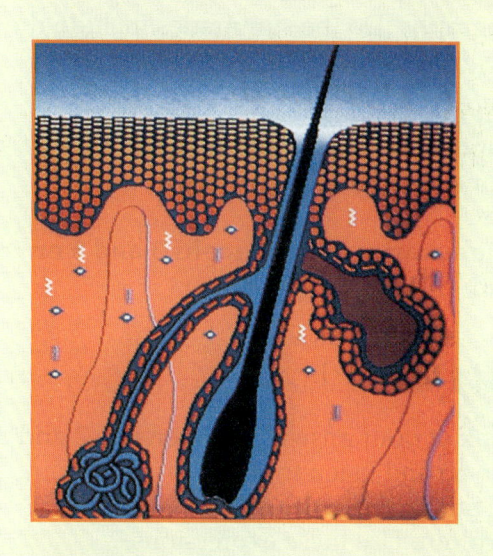

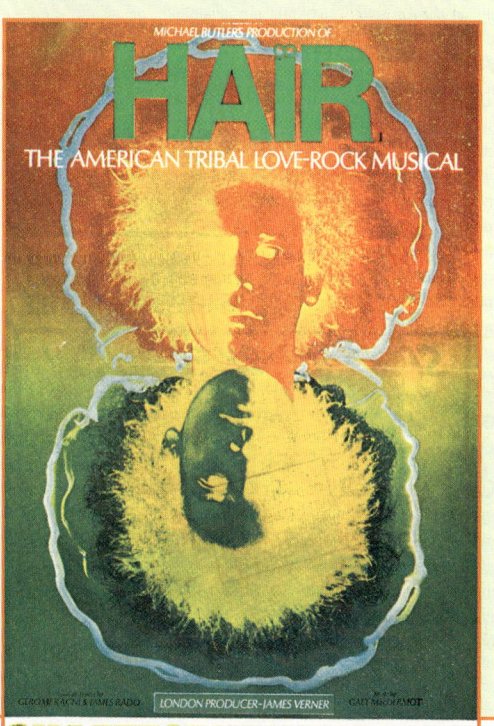

GUIDED WRITING

Summarising

1 A summary is a short version of a text which includes only the most important information.

   a Look at these summaries.

      You can change your hairstyle by wearing a wig. People have worn wigs since the time of the Ancient Egyptians.

      Hair is very versatile because you can do lots of different things with it. Your hairstyle also says a lot about you.

   b Which of the paragraphs on pages 82–3 do these texts summarise?

   c Find the topic sentences in the original paragraphs. Do the summaries include the ideas from the topic sentences?

   d What information from the original paragraphs has not been used in the summaries?

2 Write summaries of paragraphs 3 and 5 on pages 82–3.

Image

3 🔊 Look at your answers to Exercises 2 and 3 on page 80 and listen to the interview again. Write a summary of the consultant's ideas about colour. Use these expressions.

... creates an image of ...
... gives a feeling of ...
... is associated with ...

— optional activity —

Project suggestion

4 Make a project about image. Invent a new product.

- Decide what kind of image you want for the product.
- How will you create this image?
- Create possible logos, adverts, etc.

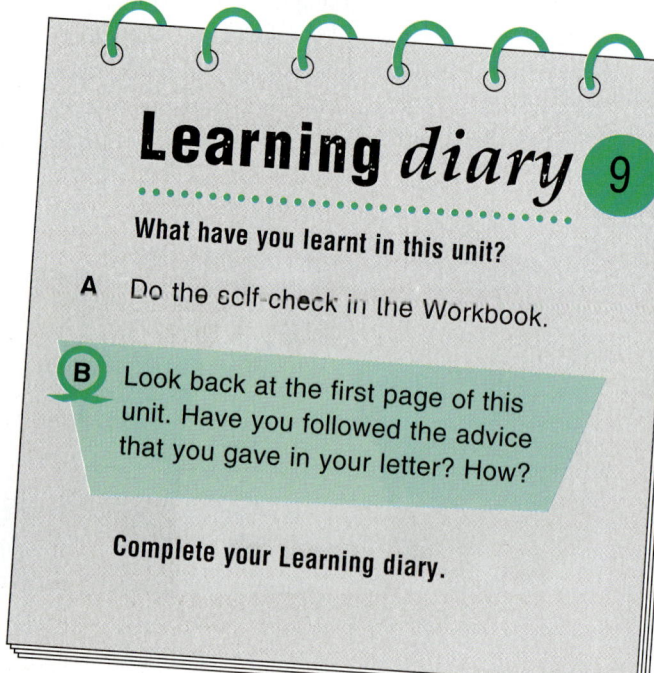

IMAGE
SPORTY ✓   YOUNG
REFRESHING   WINNERS
CLEAN   HEALTHY
PURE   EXCITING

Learning *diary* 9

What have you learnt in this unit?

A Do the self-check in the Workbook.

B Look back at the first page of this unit. Have you followed the advice that you gave in your letter? How?

Complete your Learning diary.

▶ Pronunciation: page 113

10 mistakes

Learning objectives

Learning preview: Coping with exams

Victoria Road: Expressing regret ▶ 10.1

Language work: 'should/shouldn't have' ▶ 10.1
'should/shouldn't have been ...ing' ▶ 10.1
'if' clauses (3) ▶ 10.2

Listening: Understanding a summary
have something done ▶ 10.3

Interaction: Responding appropriately
Common expressions

Reading: Understanding linking expressions
'make'/'get'/'let' ▶ 10.4

Guided writing: Linking paragraphs in a story

Learning preview: *Coping with exams*

Look at the cartoon below. What advice would you give each student.

- Finished! That was easy. I can't be bothered to check it.
- Oh no! Not reported speech! I haven't revised that. I didn't know what to revise because I couldn't remember what we'd done.
- Oh no! I didn't revise the passive! Why did I spend all that time on things I already knew?
- I've spent ten minutes on this question and I still don't know the answer. I'll never finish all the others.
- Oh, I wish I'd started my revision before last week. I was up so late last night and then I couldn't sleep because I was worried about this.
- Help! My mind's gone blank. I revised it all but now I can't remember anything. I'm going to fail.

Regrets

1 What do you remember? What happened in the last part of the story? Look back at pages 76 and 77. Check your ideas.

2 Look at the picture story. Answer these questions.

   a Where are Dan, Vince and Rosy?
   b What has happened to Kim?
   c Why is Andrea upset?
   d What does she want to do?
   e Why is Sue angry with Vince?

3 (picture 3) Anyway, it wouldn't have happened if I hadn't put my foot in it. But I didn't know she was there. And then she ran off before I could explain. And Vince was having this big argument with his boss.

Where is Vince by the way? Shouldn't he be here?

1 Do you know what happened?

It seems she took a corner too fast and the car turned over. She should have been watching the road. Luckily she was wearing her seat belt and she didn't hit anyone.

2 Vince shouldn't have let her drive in that state, you know. He should have stopped her.

Well he did try, but you know Kim.

3 🔊 Listen and follow in your book.

At the hospital

Terry How is she?

Rosy I don't know. The doctor's in with her now.

Dan Do you know what happened?

Rosy It seems she took a corner too fast and the car turned over. She should have been watching the road. Luckily she was wearing her seat belt and she didn't hit anyone.

Dan Have the police been to see her?

Rosy No, but they'll want to talk to her. She shouldn't have been driving so fast.

Terry Poor old Kim. She's really had it rough lately, hasn't she?

Dan Vince shouldn't have let her drive in that state, you know. He should have stopped her.

Terry Well he did try, but you know Kim.

Rosy Yes, she's got a very quick temper. Oh, I hope she's all right.

Terry Anyway, it wouldn't have happened if I hadn't put my foot in it. But I didn't know she was there. And then she ran off before I could explain. And Vince was having this big argument with his boss.

Dan Where is Vince by the way? Shouldn't he be here?

Terry He stormed off after he got the sack and nobody's seen him since.

VICTORIA ROAD

4 Oh, Sue. I want to go home. I shouldn't have come to England. I should have stayed in Argentina. It's all my fault.

Steady on, Andrea. What on earth is the matter? What's all your fault?

5 If I hadn't come to England, Vince wouldn't have broken up with Kim and she wouldn't have had an accident and Vince wouldn't have lost his job and ... oh, I'm so unhappy.

Come on, now. It's all right. You have a good cry and then you can tell me all about it.

6 Vince! I want a word with you!

At the Scotts' house

Sue Hi, everyone. I'm home. ... Oh, hello, Andrea.

Andrea Hi, Sue. Everyone's out.

Sue Are you all right, Andrea?

Andrea Yes, I'm OK.

Sue Well, you don't look OK. You aren't in any kind of trouble, are you?

Andrea Oh, Sue. I want to go home. I shouldn't have come to England. I should have stayed in Argentina. It's all my fault.

Sue Steady on, Andrea. What on earth is the matter? What's all your fault?

Andrea Everything would have been all right if I would stay ... no, if I stay, oh, now I can't even speak English properly.

Sue Everything would have been all right if you had stayed in Argentina. Is that what you mean?

Andrea Yes. If I hadn't come to England, Vince wouldn't have broken up with Kim and she wouldn't have had an accident and Vince wouldn't have lost his job and ... oh, I'm so unhappy.

Sue Come on, now. It's all right. You have a good cry and then you can tell me all about it.

Later

Sue Vince! I want a word with you!

What do you think?

- Will Kim be all right?
- Whose fault was the accident?
- What will Andrea do?
- What will Sue say to Vince?

4 **Right, Wrong or Don't know?**

	✓	✗	?
a Kim has had an accident.	☐	☐	☐
b She is unconscious.	☐	☐	☐
c She ran into another car.	☐	☐	☐
d Dan thinks the accident was Vince's fault.	☐	☐	☐
e Vince has been to the hospital to see Kim.	☐	☐	☐
f Andrea wants to go back to Argentina.	☐	☐	☐
g Sue already knows about Kim's accident.	☐	☐	☐

Useful expressions

5 How do you say these expressions in your language? Do you know any other English expressions with a similar meaning?

How is she?

She's had it rough.

I put my foot in it.

He stormed off.

He got the sack.

Tell me all about it.

I want a word with you!

---optional activities---

LANGUAGE USE

6 Find examples in the story of where people:

a show concern

b blame someone

c comfort someone

7 a 📼 Close your book. Listen again.

b Work in groups of three. One person is Dan and Sue, one person is Terry and the other person is Rosy and Andrea. Read the dialogue.

FOLLOW UP

8 Vince didn't know about Kim's accident. Sue had found out about it from Andrea and Terry. Sue is very angry with Vince because of all the trouble he has caused. Write their conversation. Start like this.

Sue What on earth have you been doing? When I came home ...

LANGUAGE WORK

'should / shouldn't have'

▶ 10.1

1 The sentences below are from the Victoria Road story on pages 86 and 87.

a Copy and complete them.

He .... stopped her.
I .... come to England.

We use this structure to express regret or blame.

b Translate the sentences in **a** into your own language.

2 What should or shouldn't they have done?

Example
Vince should have gone to see Kim after the picnic.

a Vince didn't go to see Kim after the picnic.
b Kim went away for the weekend.
c Kim didn't sing at the dance.
d Vince shouted at the manager.
e Kim didn't let Terry finish his story.
f Kim lost her temper.

3 These people have all done something wrong. What would their parents say to them?

Example
You shouldn't have gone out without a coat.
or *You should have worn a coat.*

a John got wet because he went out with no coat on.
b Sally and John didn't wear their crash helmets.
c Jane went out before she had finished her homework.
d David didn't practise for his piano exam and he failed.
e Pat left her car unlocked and it was stolen.
f Peter spent all his money. He had to walk home.
g Fiona forgot her appointment at the dentist.
h Clive came home late from a party.

'should / shouldn't have been ... ing' ▶ 10.1

4 Look at these sentences from the story.

She .... the road.

She .... so fast.

a Copy and complete them.

b In what tense is the verb after **should**?

c Translate the sentences into your own language.

5 Here are some reasons why accidents have happened and people have been hurt. Say what the people should or shouldn't have been doing.

Example
He shouldn't have been driving at 90 mph.

a He was driving at 90 mph.
b She wasn't wearing a seat belt.
c They were overtaking on a bend.
d He wasn't looking.
e They weren't driving carefully.
f He was driving when he was drunk.
g They were playing football in the street.
h She wasn't paying attention.

'if' clauses (3) ▶ 10.2

6 Look back at the end of the story, after Sue comes home.

a Copy and complete these sentences.

Everything .... all right, if you .... in Argentina.

If I .... to England, Vince .... with Kim.

We call these sentences unfulfilled conditions, because the events didn't actually happen.

b The tense in the main clause is called the conditional perfect. What tense is used in the **if** clause?

c We make the conditional perfect tense like this.

would/wouldn't + **have** + past participle

d Translate the sentences in **a** into your own language.

e Find more sentences like this in the story.

7 These are the events that led to Kim's accident. Say what would or wouldn't have happened if these events hadn't happened.

Examples
If Kim hadn't bought a car, they wouldn't have gone out for a picnic.
If they hadn't gone out for a picnic, Kim wouldn't have seen Vince on the ground with Andrea.

- Kim bought a car.
- They went out for a picnic.
- Kim saw Vince on the ground with Andrea.
- Kim went away for the weekend.
- She didn't sing at the dance.
- Andrea stood in for her.
- There was an argument in the shop.
- Kim lost her temper.
- She drove carelessly.
- She took a corner too fast.
- The car turned over.
- Kim was injured.

─ optional activities ─

8 Think of an incident in your life, or from a film, a book or a TV programme.

a Write down the events leading up to the incident.

b Write what would or wouldn't have happened if these events hadn't happened.

c Write what you (or the characters) should or shouldn't have done at each stage.

FOLLOW UP

9 Write your answers to Exercises 2 and 7.

LISTENING

Macbeth

1 Read this.

*'When shall we three meet again
In thunder, lightning or in rain?'*

These are the first lines of a play called *Macbeth*, which was written by William Shakespeare. The play takes place in Scotland. In the opening scenes two Scottish generals, Macbeth and Banquo, are on their way home after a battle when they meet three witches. The witches make a strange prophecy. They tell Macbeth that he will become king of Scotland. They also tell Banquo that he will not become king, but he will be the father of a king.

2 You are going to hear the story of Macbeth.

a Look at these characters from the play.

King Duncan	becomes king.
Malcolm	is killed.
Macbeth	escapes.
Lady Macbeth	goes mad and dies.
Banquo	haunts Macbeth.
Fleance	tells Macbeth to kill the king.
	comes to visit Macbeth.

b What happens to each one. Listen. Match the names to the events. Each name goes with two events.

3 a Put these events in the correct order.

A Banquo's ghost haunts Macbeth.
B The witches tell Macbeth he will be safe till the forest moves.
C Duncan visits Macbeth's castle.
D Macbeth becomes king.
E Malcolm's army attacks Dunsinane.
F Macbeth and Banquo meet the three witches.
G The witches prophesy that Macbeth will become king.
H Malcolm becomes king.
I Macbeth murders Duncan.
J Macbeth goes back to find the three witches.
K Lady Macbeth goes mad and dies.
L Macbeth is killed.
M Macbeth has Banquo murdered.

b Listen again and check your order.

have something done ▶ 10.3

4 a Look at these two sentences.

Macbeth kills Duncan.
Macbeth has Banquo killed.

In the first sentence, Macbeth kills Duncan himself. In the second sentence he doesn't do it himself. Someone does it for him. We call this a causative 'have'.

b Translate the sentences into your own language.

c Put these in the spaces below to show the structure.

object	past participle	have
_____ +	_____ +	_____ .

d Check your ideas in the Grammar reference section ▶ 10.3.

e Here are some of Macbeth's orders. Rewrite them using the structure above.

Example
He had Malcolm followed.

Follow Malcolm.
Bury the king.
Take my things to the royal palace.
Murder Banquo.
Watch the forest.

5 Answer these questions.

a Why did Macbeth murder Duncan?
b Why did he have Banquo murdered?
c Why did he believe that he was safe?
d How did the forest move?

— optional activity —

FOLLOW UP

6 Use your answers to Exercises 3 and 5. Write the story of Macbeth.

INTERACTION

Responses

1 Match the statements to the correct pictures. How would you respond to them?

A I passed my university entrance exam.
B It's my birthday today.
C I've got my driving test today.
D I don't feel very well.
E We lost 5-nil.
F Have you heard? David's in hospital.
G Happy birthday. Here's your present.
H You just stepped on my foot.

2 Look at these possible responses.

a Choose appropriate responses for the statements in Exercise 1.

b Listen and check your ideas.

1 Oh really. How did you get on?
2 Oh dear. It's nothing serious, I hope.
3 Did you have a good time?
4 Good luck. I'll keep my fingers crossed for you.
5 Have a good trip and drive safely.
6 Well, you should go home and go to bed.
7 Ooh. That sounds exciting.
8 Never mind. I'm sure you'll do better next time.
9 Well, many happy returns.
10 Oh, I'm terribly sorry. Are you all right?
11 Well done. I bet you're pleased.
12 Oh, thank you. You shouldn't have.
13 And a Happy New Year to you, too.
14 Congratulations. When's the big day?

3 Look at your dialogues. Here are some beginnings and endings for them. Choose appropriate ones to complete the dialogues.

It's all right.   You look happy.
What's the matter?   I suppose you're right.
Thank you.   You look worried.
I'm afraid I don't know.   I hope so.
Yes, I am.   Fine.
What's that?

Example
A *You look happy.*
B *I passed my university entrance exam.*
A *Well done. I bet you're pleased.*
B *Yes, I am.*

4 Work with a partner. Use your answers to Exercises 2 and 3. Say the dialogues.

—— optional activity ——

FOLLOW UP

5 Look at Exercise 2 again. You didn't use all the responses.

a Write dialogues for the unused responses.

b Role play your new dialogues with a partner.

READING

Oops!

1 Look at the texts below. There are three different stories.

   a Read the texts and decide which ones go together. There are four for each story.

   b Read the texts again. Number them in the correct order.

2 Look at your completed stories. How did you connect the different parts? What clues did you use?

A The tax inspector, however, didn't think it was very funny and a few months later the man was in court. He told the judge that the tax inspector had been too pompous. The judge told him not to be so silly in future and then let him go.

B It was ten o'clock when the two bank robbers stopped in front of the bank. But as they were getting out of the car, a traffic warden arrived. She wouldn't let the men park there, because they were on double yellow lines. So they got back into their car and drove round the corner.

C Fortunately the story has a happy ending. Before the two men had left, the shop assistant had got one of them to sign a collection note. Without thinking, the man had written his real name. The men were caught and sent to prison for two years.

D By now the men were desperate. They ran down the street. At the corner they saw a woman in a car waiting at the traffic lights. They got into the back of the car and they made the woman drive away.

E One morning in August a man went into the local tax office. He had an argument with the tax inspector, who wanted to make him pay more tax. To get his revenge the man went into the toilet at the tax office and replaced the soap with a joke soap that turned people's hands black.

F Unfortunately for the men, the woman was so frightened that she put the car into reverse and crashed into the car behind her. By now the police had arrived and the two men gave themselves up. They were charged with robbery, illegal parking and trying to steal a car.

G The assistant watched, as the men rolled up the expensive carpet and carried it to the door. She held the doors open for them as they carried it out to their van. With the carpet worth several thousand pounds on board, the men drove away.

H After the man had left there was a terrible smell of rotten eggs in the courtroom. The judge cleared the court and got the police to arrest the man again.

─── optional activity ───

WORD WORK

3 Look back through the stories.

a Find all the words and expressions in the stories associated with the law and crime.

b Use a dictionary. Find out the meaning of any that you don't know.

I It was a normal day in Carrington's department store when two men in brown overalls arrived in the carpet department. They told the assistant that they had come to collect an Indian carpet for Lord Randal.

J An hour later the man was back in the dock. He admitted dropping two stink bombs at the end of his first trial. He said that the judge had been too pompous. This time the judge made the man pay a fine of £100.

K That afternoon the poor assistant was called to the manager's office. Nobody had bought the carpet and nobody had heard of Lord Randal. The assistant shouldn't have let the men take the carpet. The two men had been stealing it.

L There was nowhere to park round the corner either, so they had to double-park. They got out and went to the bank. While they were there, an angry motorist got a policeman to call a tow-away team. When the two robbers returned, they saw their car disappearing into the distance on the back of a lorry.

'make' / 'get' / 'let' ▶ 10.4

4 Look at these sentences from the bank robbery story.

A She wouldn't .... there, because they were on double yellow lines.

B While they were there, an angry motorist .... a tow-away team.

C They got into the back of the car and they ....

a Copy and complete them.

b What is the difference in meaning between **get**, **make** and **let**? Rewrite the sentences using these expressions.

   allow ... to   force ... to   ask ... to

c When do you use **to** – with **make**, **get** or **let**?

5 Make true sentences with these cues. Use 'make', 'get', or 'let'.

a The traffic warden/the men/park somewhere else

b A police officer/a tow-away team/remove the car

c The shop assistant/the men/take the carpet

d They/her/hold the doors open for them

e The smell/the judge/clear the court

f The police/the man/go back to the courtroom

g The tax inspector/the man/pay more taxes

─── optional activity ───

FOLLOW UP

6 Work in groups. Choose one of the stories.

a Write the dialogue to make a play from the story.

b Act your play.

GUIDED WRITING

Linking paragraphs

1 Look at this story.

1 One morning in August a man went into the local tax office. He had an argument with the tax inspector, who wanted to make him pay more tax. To get his revenge the man went into the toilet at the tax office and replaced the soap with a joke soap that turned people's hands black.

2 The tax inspector, however, didn't think it was very funny and a few months later the man was in court. He told the judge that the tax inspector had been too pompous. The judge told him not to be so silly in future and let him go.

3 After the man had left, there was a terrible smell of rotten eggs in the courtroom. The judge cleared the court and got the police to arrest the man again.

4 An hour later the man was back in the dock. He admitted dropping two stink bombs at the end of his first trial. He said that the judge had been too pompous. This time the judge made the man pay a fine of £100.

a What kind of expression is used to start the story?

b How are the paragraphs linked? Look at the first sentences of paragraphs 2, 3 and 4. Find examples of these things:
- sentence linking words
- time expressions
- words repeated from the previous paragraph

c Look at the other stories on pages 92–3. What expressions are used to start them? What words or expressions are used to link the paragraphs?

The burglar

2 Look at the picture story on this page.

a What is happening in each picture?

b Write the story. Try to use some of the ideas from Exercise 1.

— optional activity —

Project suggestion

3 Think about a famous character from your country's literature. Write about him or her.

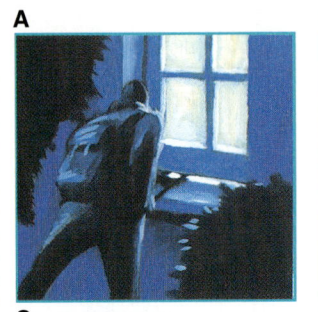

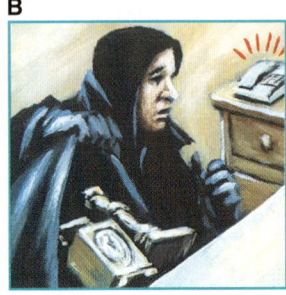

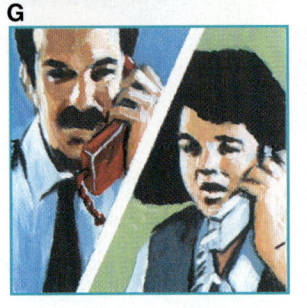

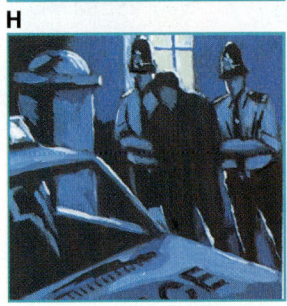

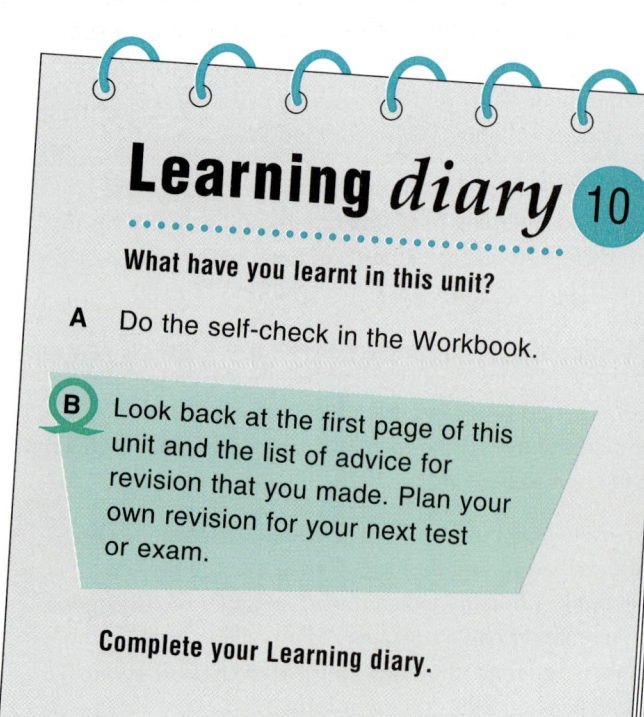

A

B

C I'm sorry. There's nobody in.

D Who am I speaking to?

E I'm the gardener.

F Why is the gardener there at night?

G

H

Learning *diary* 10

What have you learnt in this unit?

A Do the self-check in the Workbook.

B Look back at the first page of this unit and the list of advice for revision that you made. Plan your own revision for your next test or exam.

Complete your Learning diary.

▶ Pronunciation: page 113

11 fame and fortune

Learning objectives

Learning preview: How do you learn best?

Victoria Road: Talking about opportunities

Language work: Direct and indirect objects ▶ 11.1
Passive with an indirect subject ▶ 11.2

Listening: Understanding a quiz show
'one/ones' ▶ 11.3

Interaction: Role play

Reading: Persuading and giving reasons

Guided writing: Formal letters

Learning preview: *How do you learn best?*

Look at what these people say about how they learn best. Choose the three that you agree with most.

1 *Games and songs are the best. You remember the game because it's lots of fun and you sort of automatically remember the language that you had to use.*

2 *I can only learn things if I know the rule. Grammar is the most important thing to me.*

3 *I like to learn things by heart, you know, lists of words, texts, songs and poems.*

4 *I can't learn anything until I write it down, so good writing exercises are important.*

5 *Project work is a great way to learn. You make lots of mistakes but you really use the language.*

6 *Role plays and things like that. They're my favourite, because it's like you're really using the language.*

7 *I like drills and grammar exercises best. A lot of people think that they're boring, but you know what you're learning.*

8 *I find learning how to learn the most useful because then you can help yourself.*

9 *I just like to read and listen and work it out for myself.*

Decision time

1 What do you remember? What happened in the last part of the story? Look back at pages 86 and 87. Check your ideas.

2 Look at the picture story.

a What are the people talking about? Number these things to match the pictures.

- a contract
- a place at university
- Vince and Andrea
- chocolates and flowers
- the band's demo tape

b What do the people say about each thing?

3 Listen and follow in your book.

Terry Hi, Kim! We've brought you some flowers and a box of chocolates.

Kim Oh, hi, you two. This is a nice surprise. Can you give the flowers to the nurse? She'll put them in a vase. But you can give the chocolates to me. Mmm, my favourites.

Terry How are you feeling?

Kim Much better, thanks. I've had lots of visitors. Even Andrea's been to see me. She brought me those roses over there. She came with Vince's sister, Sue. She's down for the summer.

Terry Yes, I know. ... Er Kim, I don't know if I should say this, but do you know about Vince and Andrea? They're ... well, you know ... er ...

Kim Oh, don't worry. I know all about it. I've had a lot of time to think while I've been here. Andrea told me that she was going back to Argentina for the summer.

Rosy Yeah, that's right. She might be back in October though. She's been offered a place at Edinburgh University. But she doesn't know whether to accept it now. She wanted somewhere closer to Hartfield.

Kim Closer to Vince, you mean.

Rosy Well, that may be difficult with our bit of news.

Kim What news is that?

We've been to London today to see the agent that was at the dance. Terry had already told him that Andrea wasn't our real singer. That was why he wanted to see us again. Well, we explained that you were in hospital and so, you know that demo tape that we made a few weeks ago? We gave it to him and he listened to it.

Well, what did he think? Come on. Don't keep me in suspense. What did he say?

Hi, Kim! We've brought you some flowers and a box of chocolates.

Oh, hi, you two. This is a nice surprise. Can you give the flowers to the nurse? She'll put them in a vase. But you can give the chocolates to me. Mmm, my favourites.

Kim, I don't know if I should say this, but do you know about Vince and Andrea? They're ... well, you know ... er ...

Oh, don't worry. I know all about it. I've had a lot of time to think while I've been here.

VICTORIA ROAD

Terry We've got it all sorted out about the band.

Kim What do you mean?

Rosy We've been to London today to see the agent that was at the dance. Terry had already told him that Andrea wasn't our real singer. That was why he wanted to see us again. Well, we explained that you were in hospital and so, you know that demo tape that we made a few weeks ago? We gave it to him and he listened to it.

Kim Well, what did he think? Come on. Don't keep me in suspense. What did he say?

Terry Shall I tell her?

Rosy Yes, go on.

Terry He thought you had a great voice. But here's the best bit. He's offered us a contract for one of the tours that he's arranging for the autumn. It's on a cruise round the Mediterranean running from the beginning of October to Christmas.

Kim Oh, isn't it exciting? We're going to be rich and famous. What do the others think?

Rosy Dan thinks it's great. We haven't spoken to Vince yet.

At the Scott's house

Sue Who's your letter from, Vince?

Vince It's from Nottingham University. They want to know if I'm going to take up the place they offered me last year. If I don't take it up this year, they'll offer it to someone else and I'll have to apply again.

Mr Scott Well, there's no question of that, is there? Why wouldn't you take it up this year?

What do you think?

- What will Andrea decide?
- What will Vince do?
- How will other people react?

4 Copy and complete these sentences with the correct subjects.

a .... brought Kim some roses.

b .... went to the hospital with Andrea.

c .... knows about Vince and Andrea.

d .... have been to see the recording agent.

e .... has offered the band a contract.

f .... runs from October to Christmas.

g .... doesn't know about the contract yet.

h .... expects Vince to go to Nottingham.

Useful expressions

5 How do you say these expressions in your language? Do you know any other English expressions with a similar meaning?

How are you feeling?

I don't know if I should say this.

our bit of news

We've got it all sorted out.

Don't keep me in suspense.

There's no question of that.

---optional activities---

LANGUAGE USE

6 Find some examples of where people:

a ask for clarification

b express pleasure

7 a 📼 Close your book. Listen again.

b Work in groups of three. One person is Rosy and Sue. One person is Terry and Mr Scott. One person is Kim and Vince. Read the dialogue.

FOLLOW UP

8 Answer these questions.

a What have Rosy and Terry brought Kim?
b How does Kim feel about Vince and Andrea?
c Why might Andrea come back to Britain?
d Why have Rosy and Terry been to London today?
e What was the result of their visit to London?
f What do the band members think about the news?
g What must Vince decide about Nottingham?

LANGUAGE WORK

Direct and indirect objects

▶ 11.1

1 The sentence below is from the Victoria Road story on pages 96 and 97.

a Copy and complete it.

Can you give .... to .... ?

the flowers are the direct object. Someone gave them.
the nurse is the indirect object. She will receive them.

b What word introduces the indirect object?

c Find more examples of indirect objects in the story.

2 Complete these sentences with the words in brackets in the correct order.

Example
Shirley gave the agent's address to Terry.

a Shirley gave (Terry/the agent's address/to)
b Rosy and Terry wrote (to/a letter/the agent)
c They sent (his secretary/to/their demo tape)
d The secretary gave (him/it/to)
e The agent has offered (to/a contract/the band) He will send (Rosy/to/it)

3 Now look at two more sentences from the story.

She brought .... over there.

He's offered .... for one of the tours.

a Copy and complete them.

b Put a circle round the direct objects and a box round the indirect objects in the sentences in **a**.

c Copy and complete this rule.

> If we put 'to' in front of the indirect object, it goes _____ the direct object.
> If we don't put 'to' in front of the indirect object, it goes _____ the direct object.
> Note: when the direct object is a pronoun, we normally put it first, so the indirect object must have 'to'.

4 Use the cues in Exercise 2. Make the sentences without 'to' wherever possible.

Example
Shirley gave Terry the agent's address.

5 What is happening in these pictures? Use these verbs.

write   give   offer   send   serve   lend

Example
The pupils are giving the teacher their homework.
or
The pupils are giving their homework to the teacher.

— optional activity —

6 Look at the rule in Exercise 3c.

a Look at this sentence: *I gave a book to Terry.*

b 🔊 Listen. Change the sentence with the cues that you hear.

Examples
'to Kim' → *I gave a book to Kim.*
'some flowers' → *I gave some flowers to Kim.*
'Andrea' → *I gave Andrea some flowers.*

Passive with an indirect subject ▶ 11.2

7 Look at these sentences. Copy them.

Active: Edinburgh University has offered Andrea a place.
Passive: Andrea has been offered a place by Edinburgh University.

a In the active sentence, put a circle round the direct object and a box round the indirect object.

b Now look at the passive sentence. Which object has become the subject of the passive verb?

c Translate the sentences.

d Copy and complete this rule.

> If an active sentence has both a direct object and an indirect object, we normally use the _____ object to form the subject of the passive.

8 Change these sentences so that the indirect object becomes the subject.

Example
Kim has been given lots of cards.

a Lots of cards have been given to Kim.
b A university place has been offered to Andrea.
c A letter has been sent to Vince.
d His place will be offered to someone else.
e A contract has been offered to the band.
f Some flowers were given to Kim.
g Hundreds of demo tapes are sent to the agent.

— optional activity —

FOLLOW UP

9 Write your answers to Exercises 2, 4 and 8.

LISTENING

Quiz show time!

1 Look at these people. What do you think is happening?

2 Look at these names.

June Bride   Halifax   Fred Bare   Penny Farthing
Leeds   Wally Brain   Norwich   Sandy Beach

a 📼 Listen to the first part of the tape.

b What is the name of the show?

c Match the names and the places to the people in the picture.

3 📼 Who do you want to win? Listen to the whole of the tape.

a Who comes first, second and third?

b What prize does each person win?

4 Here are the expressions that the contestants had to complete.

a Copy and complete them.

b 📼 Listen again and check your answers.

c Have you got similar expressions in your language?

- as green as _____
- as heavy as _____
- as cool as _____
- as dry as _____

- bread and _____
- night and _____
- horse and _____
- king and _____

- Pride comes before a _____
- Easy come _____
- Penny wise and _____
  _____

'one / ones' ▶ 11.3

5 Look at these sentences from the tape.

Wally I want you to complete each expression. So your first .... will be 'as green as'.

Wally Which questions do you want – the red questions, the blue questions or the yellow questions?

June I'll have the yellow .... , please, Wally.

a What words are missing from the gaps?
b What do **one** and **ones** refer to?
c Translate the sentences.

6 Look at the list of choices below. Which one(s) would you choose? Work in pairs. Ask and answer.

Example
A *Would you choose a gold ring or a silver ring?*
B *I'd choose a gold one.*

a gold ring or a silver ring
tight jeans or baggy jeans
a red T-shirt or a blue T-shirt
a serious book or a funny book
dark clothes or light clothes
an English test or a Maths test
white trainers or black trainers

---
optional activities

W O R D   W O R K

7 Words from the quiz show

a What are these things?

host   jackpot
hostess   prize
contestants score
round

b What do you think **empty-handed** means?

8 Work in groups of five. Role play the show.

---
optional activity

FOLLOW UP

9 Copy and complete what Wally says.

So I'm .... we have to .... goodbye to you .... It's been great .... you on the .... You've been a .... contestant. And you won't go away .... Sandy will tell you what you have ....

Don't worry. Just .... calm and you'll .... all right. Now I'm .... to give you three .... proverbs. After I have read each ...., I want you to give .... the complete .... You've got fifteen .... If you complete them .... in fifteen seconds, you'll take home our .... of £5,000. The fifteen seconds .... now.

INTERACTION

Your quiz show

1 Discuss these questions.

a Which is your favourite quiz show? Why?
b What sorts of prizes can people win?
c What must they do?

2 Make your own 'Win or Lose' show. Work in groups of five.

a Write some questions for the second round and the jackpot round. You can make any kind of questions – general knowledge questions, questions about English, questions about a sport or a pop star, etc.

b Choose one person to be Wally, one to be Sandy and the other three to be contestants.

c Exchange questions with another group. Only Wally should see the questions.

d Act your show.

---
optional activity

FOLLOW UP

3 Write part of the dialogue from your show.

READING

1 Look at this text.
  a What is it about?
  b Where is it from?

Champions

It's time once again for our annual Champion of the Year award. Every year we invite you, our readers, to write and tell us about someone who you think has helped to make life better for other people. We don't want famous people, but ordinary men and women, boys and girls, who in some small way have made the world a happier place. It might be a member of your family, a neighbour, a friend, a teacher. If you would like to nominate someone, we want to hear from you. Write and tell us who you would like to nominate and why.

Write to   Valerie Stubbs
            Editor
            Teen Scene
            16 Harwood Place
            London SW18 4BK

All letters must be received by 19 October.

2 Read the text again. Answer these questions.
  1 How often is the award given?
  2 What do readers have to do?
  3 What kind of people can't you nominate?
  4 What should the people you nominate have done?
  5 Who must you write to?
  6 When is the closing date?

3 Here are three letters that the editor received.
  a Copy this chart.

1 Letter	2 Writer	3 Person nominated	4 Reason
A			
B			
C			

  b Complete columns 2 and 3 with the names.
  c Complete column 4. Choose from this list.

  helped to protect the environment
  saved a life
  has worked very hard
  helps homeless people
  rescued a dog
  has made people's lives easier

  d What relationship is each person nominated to the writer?

A

> Green Bank Farm
> Wellet
> Kent
> CT4 2LR
>
> 5 October
>
> Valerie Stubbs
> Editor
> Teen Scene
> 16 Harwood Place
> London SW18 4BK
>
> Dear Ms Stubbs
>
> I would like to nominate someone for the Champion of the Year award. The person I would like to nominate is a teacher at our school. Her name is Sharon Lynch.
>
> This summer Mrs Lynch spent her summer holiday walking from our school to Land's End and back – about 600 miles – in order to raise money for charity. With the £5000 that she raised, the local community centre was able to buy a minibus, which will be used to take sports teams to competitions and to bring old and handicapped people to the centre.
>
> Mrs Lynch's walk has helped to make a lot of people's lives easier and more interesting. That's why I think she should be Champion of the Year.
>
> Yours sincerely
> *Angela Barton*
> Angela Barton

B

11 West Street
London SE7 5TG
2 October

Valerie Stubbs
Editor
Teen Scene
16 Harwood Place
London SW18 4BK

Dear Valerie

I would like to nominate our dog, Scruff, for the Champion of the Year award. I know he's not a person, but he has certainly made our lives happier in the past year.

Last March my little brother, Ben, took Scruff for a walk. They should have been home for tea, but by 7 o'clock it was getting dark and they still hadn't returned. My parents were very worried and they called the police. They finally found Ben, because they heard Scruff barking. Ben had fallen down an old mine and was unconscious. The police said that if Scruff hadn't stayed with Ben, they would never have found him in time.

Ben is now OK and we have Scruff to thank for that. That's why I think Scruff should be Champion of the Year.

Yours sincerely

John Bond
John Bond

---

5 Carlton Avenue
Glasgow D7 9BR

30 September

Valerie Stubbs
Editor
Teen Scene
16 Harwood Place
London SW18 4BK

Dear Valerie

I would like to nominate my friend for your Champion award. His name is Andrew Ringer and he's 17 years old.

Although he is studying for his A-levels, Andrew gives up most of his free time to help homeless young people in our city. Every weekend he works at a centre which provides food and a bed for them.

If it weren't for people like Andrew, these people would have to spend the night on the streets with nothing to eat. That's why I think he should get the award.

Yours sincerely,

David Macintosh
David Macintosh

---

4 Answer these questions.

a What is unusual about John's nomination?
b What happened to Ben?
c How did Scruff save his life?
d How far did Mrs Lynch walk?
e What will the minibus be used for?
f How old is Andrew?
g Is he still at school?
j When does he go to the centre?

— optional activities —

W O R D   W O R K

5 Match the items in columns A and B. For some of the verbs there is more than one possibility.

A	B
get	the night
give	dark
call	for a walk
fall	up
spend	for an exam
study	down
take	the police

6 What do you think?

a If you were judging the letters, what criteria would you use to help you decide?

b Do any of these nominees deserve the award?

c If these were the three finalists, which one would you choose? Why?

FOLLOW UP

7 Use your answers to Exercises 3 and 4. Write a summary of each of the letters.

Example
John Bond wants to nominate his dog, Scruff, because he saved his brother Ben's life. Ben fell down an old mine, but Scruff stayed with him and the police were able to find him.

GUIDED WRITING

Formal letters

▼ 1 **Look at the letter.**

a Match the letters (A–G) to these things.

receiver's name
greeting
sender's name
sender's address
sender's signature
date
receiver's address

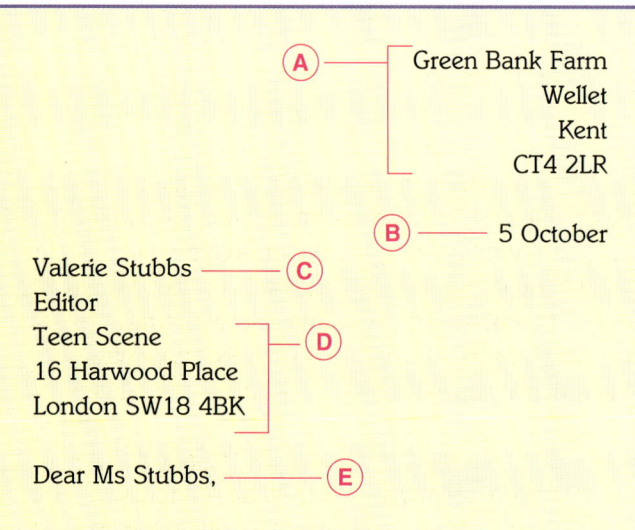

b What expression is used to end the letter?

c Compare the letter to the personal letter on page 26. What differences are there?

d Look at all the letters on pages 102–3. One of these forms of greeting is not correct. Which one?

Dear Valerie Dear Ms Stubbs
Dear Valerie Stubbs

▼ 2 **The letter has three paragraphs. Put these in the correct order to match the paragraphs.**

What has the person done?
How do the person's actions justify the nomination?
Who would you like to nominate?

Your letter

▼ 3 **Write your own letter to nominate someone for the Champion of the Year award. Use the ideas from Exercises 1 and 2.**

— optional activity —

Project suggestion

▼ 4 **Work in a group. Put your letters together and choose a Champion of the Year. Produce the magazine page announcing the winner and runners-up.**

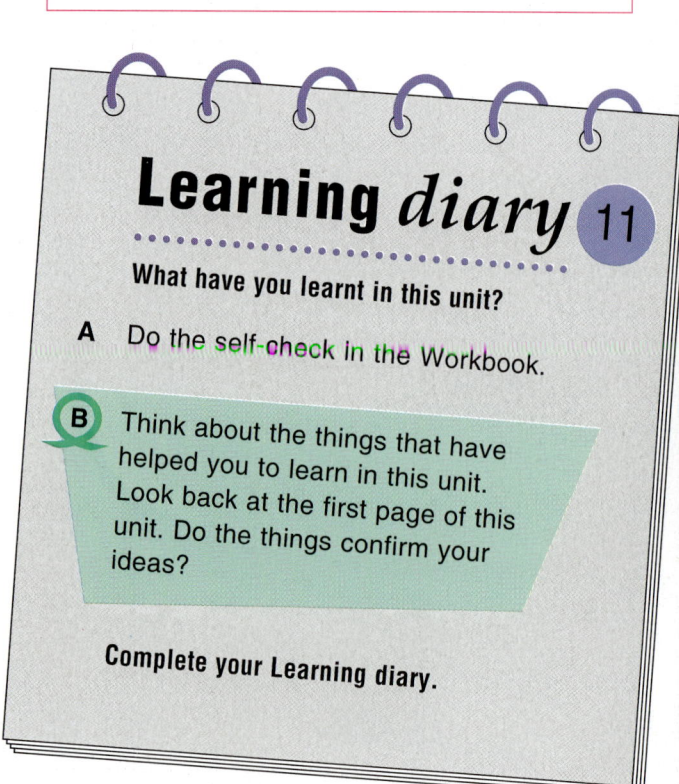

A — Green Bank Farm
Wellet
Kent
CT4 2LR

B — 5 October

Valerie Stubbs — C
Editor
Teen Scene — D
16 Harwood Place
London SW18 4BK

Dear Ms Stubbs, — E

I would like to nominate someone for the Champion of the Year award. The person I would like to nominate is a teacher at our school. Her name is Sharon Lynch.

This summer Mrs Lynch spent her summer holiday walking from our school to Land's End and back – about 600 miles – in order to raise money for charity. With the £5000 that she raised, the local community centre was able to buy a minibus, which will be used to take sports teams to competitions and to bring old and handicapped people to the centre.

Mrs Lynch's walk has helped to make a lot of people's lives easier and more interesting. That's why I think she should be Champion of the Year.

Yours sincerely,

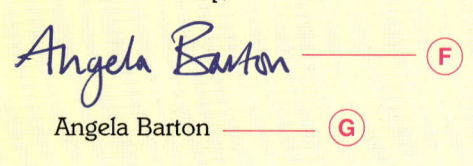

Angela Barton — F

Angela Barton — G

Learning diary 11

What have you learnt in this unit?

A Do the self-check in the Workbook.

B Think about the things that have helped you to learn in this unit. Look back at the first page of this unit. Do the things confirm your ideas?

Complete your Learning diary.

▶ Pronunciation: page 113

revision 12

1 reading skills / grammar

1 Look at the pictures.
  a Put them in the correct order to make a story.
  b Read the text and check your order.

2 a Read the text again. Choose the correct alternatives to complete it.

A chance in a million

A few years ago Margaret Powdrill was **in/on** a plane from New York to London. She **is/was** sitting next to a businessman from Israel and they started **talking/talk** to each other. She asked him why **was he/he was** going to London, and he **told/said** her that he was only changing planes there. He said that he **is/was** going to Tel Aviv for a family reunion, and he showed **to her/her** a photograph of his family.

Suddenly in her mind Margaret saw a plane **fell/falling** from the sky. She knew it was the man's plane. **Although/However** she felt a bit stupid, she told the man **not to/to not** catch the plane. At first the man did not believe her, but finally she **let/got** him to change his ticket. He should **have taken/take** a flight the same day, but he had **changed the ticket/the ticket changed** to the next day's flight, and booked into a hotel at the airport for the night.

Margaret was **living/staying** at the same hotel and that evening they went out to dinner together. The man was still not sure **whether/weather** he had done the right thing.

  b 📼 Listen and check your text.

3 Did the man do the right thing?
  a How do you think the story ends?
  b 📼 Listen to the rest of the story and find out.

4 Copy and complete these sentences with the words in brackets.

a If Margaret .... the man, she .... the plane falling. (*not meet/not see*)

b If Margaret .... him about it, he .... his flight. (*not tell/not change*)

c If the plane ...., he .... very stupid. (*not crash/feel*)

d If he .... Margaret, he .... (*not believe/die*)

5 Look at these dialogues.

a Copy and complete them.

b Match them to the correct pictures in Exercise 1.

c Make a dialogue for the ending of the story.

A I'm still not sure I've done the right thing. It's nice to have dinner with you, but I shouldn't have .... I should .... today. If the plane ...., I'll feel pretty stupid.

B Why .... London?
I'm ....

C I'm .... for a family reunion. Would you like ....?

D I know this sounds stupid, but I've just .... You mustn't .... You should ....

E Can I help you?
Yes, please. I'd like ....
I see. When ....?
....

---- optional activity ----

6 The story is true.

a Do you think Margaret really saw his plane crashing or was it just coincidence?

b Do you know of any strange coincidences?

c If you could see into the future, what would you want to know?

2 listening skills / reading skills

1 Look at the song.

a What do you think the missing words are?

b 🔊 Listen and check your ideas.

Oh Boy!

All of my ...., all of .... kissin'
You don't .... what you've been a-............
Oh Boy when .... with me
Oh Boy the world can ....
That you .... meant for me.

.... of my life I've .... a-waitin'
.... there'll be .... hesitatin'
Oh Boy .... you're with me
Oh Boy the .... can see
That you were .... for me.

.... appear and the shadows .... fallin'
I .... hear my .... a-callin'
A .... bit of lovin' makes .... right
And .... gonna see my .... tonight.

Epilogue

1 What happened in the last part of the story? Look back at pages 96 and 97. Check your ideas.

2 What will the various characters do?
a Write a final episode for Victoria Road.
b Role play your dialogue.

3 Look at the pictures of the characters.
a 📼 Listen. What happens to each of the characters?
b Compare the ending with your own story.

— optional activity —

4 Use the information in Exercise 3. Write a summary of what has happened to the Victoria Road characters since Kim's accident.

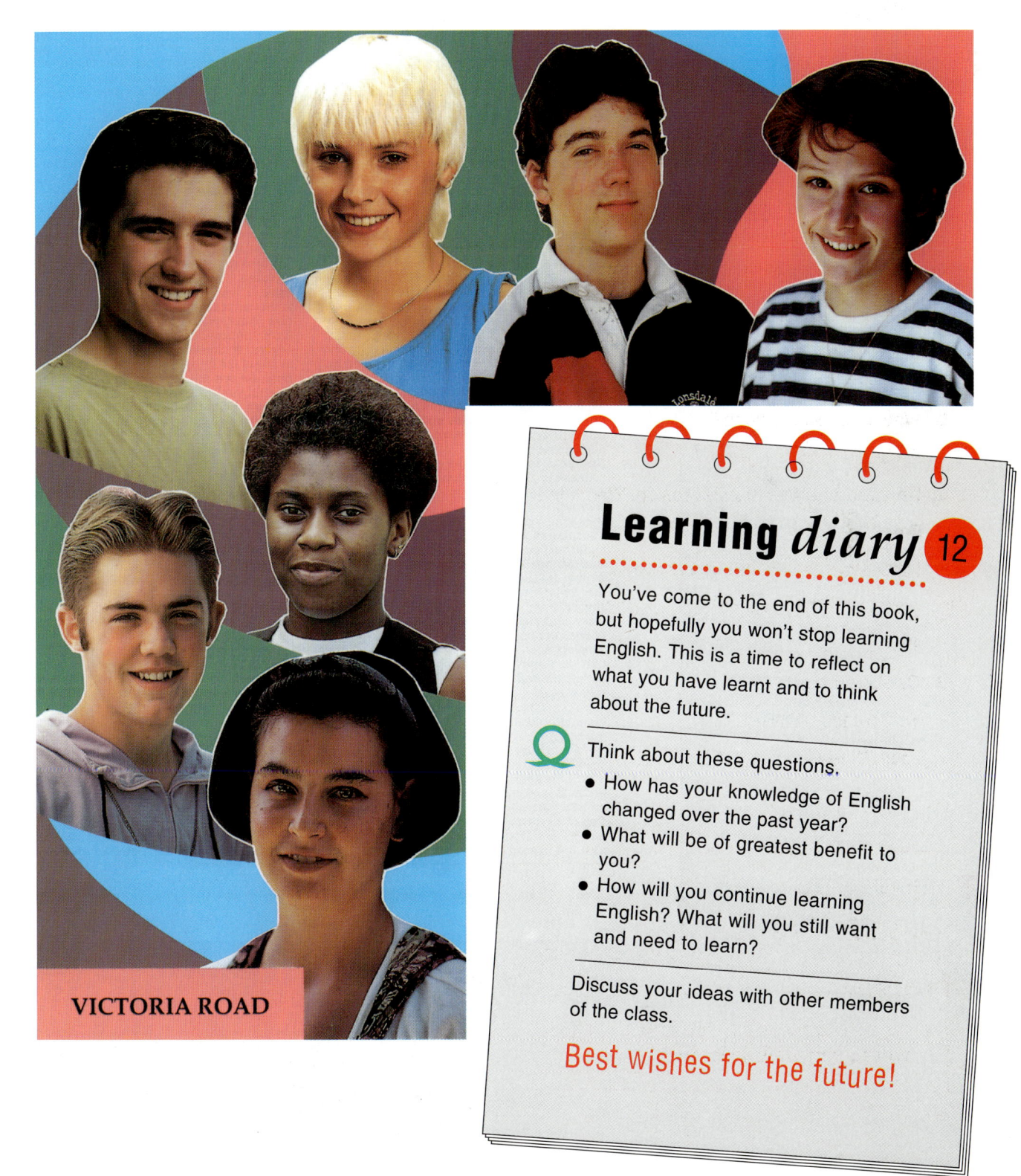

VICTORIA ROAD

Learning *diary* 12

You've come to the end of this book, but hopefully you won't stop learning English. This is a time to reflect on what you have learnt and to think about the future.

Think about these questions.
- How has your knowledge of English changed over the past year?
- What will be of greatest benefit to you?
- How will you continue learning English? What will you still want and need to learn?

Discuss your ideas with other members of the class.

Best wishes for the future!

▶ Pronunciation: page 113

Dictionary page

- different meanings of the same part of speech
- The word can be more than one part of speech.
- a note about grammar or use
- This sign by a headword shows words that are more important to learn.
- a countable noun
- pronunciation
- the part of speech

an example sentence showing the word in use

This mark is placed in front of the syllable which is stressed.

an uncountable noun

The verb can be intransitive (it has no object) or transitive (it must have an object).

You will find the meaning under this word.

a different spelling, meaning, pronunciation or use in American English

finish — firm

part of sth: *Finish up your milk, Tom!* 3 [T] **finish sth (off)** to complete the last details of sth or make sth perfect: *He's just adding the finishing touches to his painting.* ○ *He stayed up all night to finish off the article he was writing.* (PHRASAL VERBS) **finish sb/sth off** (*informal*) to kill sb/sth: *The cat pounced and finished off the mouse.* ○ (*figurative*) *It was losing his job that really finished him off* (= depressed him). **finish with sb/sth 1** to stop needing or using sb/sth: *Don't go away, I haven't finished with you yet.* ○ *I'll borrow that book when you've finished with it.* **2** to end a relationship with sb: *Sally's not going out with David any more – she finished with him last month.*

finish² /ˈfɪnɪʃ/ *noun* [C] **1** (used especially about a race) the end: *The last race was a very close finish* (= the runners at the front were close together at the end). ☛ The opposite is **start**. **2** (used especially about wood and furniture) the feel or look that sth has when it has been polished, etc: *This table has a beautiful finish.*

☆ **finished** /ˈfɪnɪʃt/ *adj* **1** (not before a noun) **finished (with sb/sth)** having stopped doing sth, using sth or dealing with sb/sth: *'Are you using the computer?' 'Yes, I won't be finished with it for another hour or so.'* **2** (not before a noun) not able to continue: *The business is finished – there's no more money.* **3** made; completed: *the finished product, article, etc*

fiord (*also* **fjord**) /ˈfjɔːd/ *noun* [C] a long narrow piece of sea between cliffs, especially in Norway

fir /fɜː(r)/ (*also* **ˈfir-tree**) *noun* [C] a straight tree that keeps its thin leaves (**needles**) in winter

ˈfir-cone *noun* [C] the fruit of the fir

☆ **fire¹** /ˈfaɪə(r)/ *noun* **1** [U] hot bright flames produced by sth that is burning: *Many animals are afraid of fire.* **2** [C,U] burning that destroys and is out of control: *Firemen struggled for three hours to put out the fire.* ○ *It had been a dry summer so there were many forest fires.* ○ *You need to insure your house against fire.* ○ *The furniture caught fire within seconds* (= started burning). ○ *Did someone set fire to that pile of wood?* ○ *Help! The frying-pan's on fire!* **3** [C] burning wood or coal to warm people or cook food: *They lit a fire to keep warm.* ○ *It's cold – don't let the fire go out!* ○ *a camp fire* ○ *Many older houses have an open fire in the sitting-room.* **4** [C] an apparatus for heating a room, etc: *a gas fire* ○ *an electric fire* **5** [U] shooting from guns: *The soldiers were under fire from all sides.* ○ *I could hear gunfire in the distance.* (IDIOM) **open fire** ⇨ OPEN²

ˈfire-alarm *noun* [C] a bell or other signal to warn people that there is a fire: *If the fire-alarm goes off, leave the building immediately.*

ˈfirearm *noun* [C, usually pl] a gun that you can carry: *Most policemen don't carry firearms.*

ˈfire brigade (*US* **ˈfire department**) *noun* [C, with sing or pl verb] an organization of people trained to put out (= stop) fires: *Dial 999 to call the fire brigade.*

ˈfire-engine *noun* [C] a special vehicle that carries equipment for fighting large fires

ˈfire escape *noun* [C] a special staircase on the outside of a building that people can escape down if there is a fire

ˈfire extinguisher (*also* **extinguisher**) *noun* [C] a metal container with water or chemicals inside that you use for fighting small fires: *Shops and offices have fire extinguishers on every floor.*

ˈfire-fighter *noun* [C] a person who fights fires

ˈfirelight *noun* [U] the light that comes from a fire in a fireplace: *It's quite romantic sitting here in the firelight.*

ˈfireman /-mən/ *noun* [C] (*pl* **firemen** /-mən/) a person whose job is to fight fires: *Firemen have to wear special uniforms.*

ˈfireplace *noun* [C] the open place in a room (at the bottom of a chimney) where you light a fire

ˈfireside *noun* [C, usually sing] the part of a room beside the fireplace: *Come and sit by the fireside.*

ˈfire station *noun* [C] a building where fire-engines are kept and firemen wait to be called

ˈfirewood *noun* [U] wood used for lighting or burning on fires

fire² /ˈfaɪə(r)/ *verb* **1** [I,T] **fire (sth) (at sb/sth); fire (sth) into sth** to shoot with a gun or shoot bullets, etc from a gun: *'Fire!' shouted the officer.* ○ *Can you hear the guns firing?* ○ *He fired his gun at the ceiling.* ○ *They fired rubber bullets into the crowd.* **2** [T] (*informal*) to dismiss sb from a job: *He was fired for always being late.* **3** [T] **fire sth at sb** to ask questions, or make remarks, quickly and aggressively: *If you stop firing questions at me I might be able to answer!* **4** [T] **fire sb with sth** to produce a strong feeling in sb: *Her speech fired me with determination.*

-fired (in compounds) using the fuel mentioned: *gas-fired central heating*

ˈfiring-squad *noun* [C] a group of soldiers who have been ordered to shoot and kill a prisoner

firework /ˈfaɪəwɜːk/ *noun* [C] a small container with chemicals inside that burns or explodes with coloured lights and bangs, used for entertainment: *Be careful not to burn your fingers when you let off that firework.* ○ *a firework display/party*

☛ **Firework** is often used in the plural: *We went to watch the fireworks in Hyde Park.*

☆ **firm¹** /fɜːm/ *noun* [C, with sing or pl verb] a business company: *Which firm do you work for?* ○ *My firm's moving to Manchester soon.*

☆ **firm²** /fɜːm/ *adj* **1** able to stay the same shape when pressed; quite hard: *a firm mattress* **2** strong or steady or not likely to change: *She kept a firm grip on her mother's hand.* ○ *Have*

ɜː	ə	eɪ	əʊ	aɪ	aʊ	ɔɪ	ɪə	eə	ʊə
fur	ago	pay	home	five	now	join	near	hair	pure

Sample pages from the *Oxford Wordpower Dictionary*

PRONUNCIATION PRACTICE

Introduction
Phonetic alphabet: revision

1 a ▶ These are the vowel sounds of English. Listen and repeat.

/iː/	seen	/juː/	museum
/ɪ/	sit	/ɜː/	bird
/e/	pet	/ə/	trainers
/æ/	fan	/eɪ/	stay
/ɑː/	half	/aɪ/	time
/ʌ/	cut	/ɔɪ/	noise
/ɒ/	what	/aʊ/	now
/ɔː/	door	/əʊ/	both
/ʊ/	would	/eə/	where
/uː/	do	/ɪə/	clear

b Write one more word for each of the sounds.

2 These are the consonant sounds of English. Match the words in the box with the sounds.

/d/ .... /ʃ/ .... /ð/ .... /h/ ....
/t/ .... /tʃ/ .... /θ/ .... /m/ ....
/b/ .... /ʒ/ .... /s/ .... /n/ ....
/p/ .... /dʒ/ .... /ŋ/ .... /l/ ....
/g/ .... /f/ .... /j/ .... /r/ ....
/k/ .... /v/ .... /z/ .... /w/ ....

sheep	history	wrong	which
can	get	last	treasure
village	choose	cheese	boring
take	your	think	brown
new	disk	put	mother
feel	move	case	river

3 What are these words?

/ʃɔːts/ /wɜːs/
/dʒʌst/ /θrəʊ/
/ˈfæktərɪ/ /ðiːz/
/kætʃ/ /sɒŋ/

Unit 1
-ty or -teen?

1 a ▶ Look at these numbers. Listen and repeat them.

```
18    13    50    70    17
 •     •     •     •     •

16    80    90    15    30
 •     •     •     •     •

40    60    14    19    20
 •     •     •     •     •
```

b Copy the pattern of numbers and dots.

c ▶ Listen. Join the dots in the order that you hear the numbers. If you join them correctly, you'll see how old Dan was when he first started playing the drums.

Unit 2
Reduced vowels

2 a ▶ In faster speech some vowels are reduced to an /ə/ sound. Listen.

/wɒt wɒz ɪt laɪk/ (What was it like?)
becomes
/wɒt wəz ɪt laɪk/

/juːnəʊ/ (You know.)
becomes
/jənəʊ/

As a general rule we reduce vowels in words that do not carry a lot of the meaning of the sentence.

b Look at these sentences. Where will there be /ə/ sounds in fast speech?

We've got to go.
We were there for two years.
I'd like a sandwich and a cup of tea.
Are you from Hungary?
Where does he live?
What colour eyes has she got?
I was at the airport for five hours.

c ▶ Listen. Check your ideas.

d ▶ Listen again and repeat.

Unit 3
Syllable stress

1 a When a word has more than one syllable, one of the syllables is usually stressed more than the other(s).

> Examples
> mo•dern   elec•tric

b 📼 Listen. Which syllable is stressed?

equipment	cosmetics	performance
acoustic	together	number
Thursday	other	famous

2 Look at the words above.

a Where does the stress usually fall:
- in words with two syllables?
- in words with three syllables?

b Find more words that follow this pattern in the dictionary extract on pages 108 and 109.

3 📼 Not all words follow these patterns. Listen. Which syllable is stressed in these words?

probably	video	hospital
suppose	express	volunteer
guitar	telephone	negative

Don't forget to check the pronunciation of a new word in a dictionary.

4 📼 Listen again and repeat all the words in Exercises 1b and 3.

Unit 4
Vowels: revision

1 📼 Listen. Which word do you hear 1 or 2?

	1	2		1	2
A	mean	men	F	want	won't
B	now	no	G	had	hard
C	work	walk	H	take	talk
D	can	can't	I	first	fast
E	wheel	will	J	live	leave

2 📼 Which word doesn't rhyme?

A	mean	seen	dead
B	talk	calm	arm
C	wait	said	hate
D	look	room	soon
E	door	good	more
F	come	home	some
G	you	through	your
H	glass	bass	place

Unit 5
Silent letters

1 a Some words have letters which are not pronounced. Look at this list of words. What are the silent letters?

unknown	write	whisper	castle
guess	tongue	could	scissors
science	talk	knife	thumb
island	wrong	answer	parliament
who	rhythm	climb	hour

b 📼 Listen and check your ideas.

c 📼 Listen again and repeat.

Unit 6
Intonation of question tags

1 Listen and follow in your book.

Question tags sometimes have a falling intonation and sometimes a rising intonation. The meaning is different.

A falling intonation means that we think the statement is true and we expect the other person to agree.

> Example
> You like travelling, *don't you?* ↘

We use a rising intonation when we are not sure of the answer. It's more like a real question.

> Examples
> You aren't getting a cold, *are you?* ↗
>
> Kim isn't leaving, *is she?* ↗

2 a 🔊 **Listen to these examples. Does the intonation rise or fall on the question tag?**

   A You're Sue Scott's penfriend, aren't you?
   Yes, I am.

   Sue's at Oxford now, isn't she?
   Yes, that's right.

   B We aren't practising tonight, are we?
   No. It's Sunday.

   Oh, good. We're meeting at Vince's place, aren't we?
   Yes, at eight o'clock.

   C You haven't seen my song book, have you?
   No. You lent it to Terry, didn't you?
   Oh yes, so I did.

   D Terry Moore lives next door to you, doesn't he?
   Yes, that's right.

   He isn't still away, is he?
   No, he's been back a few weeks now.

   E We'll have to get the six o'clock train, won't we?
   Yes, and you won't forget the tickets, will you?
   Oh, thanks for reminding me.

   b Listen again and repeat.

Unit 7
Word linking

1 a When we speak, we often run words together. This makes speech sound smoother. Here are some of the ways that this can happen.

   1 When there is a consonant sound on the end of a word and the next word starts with a vowel sound, the consonant runs on to the vowel so that there is no break between the words.

   Example
   I'm not going to sulk about it.

   Where are the links in these sentences?

   But what about Saturday?
   She said that was our problem.
   We'll soon find out.

   b 🔊 **Now listen and repeat.**

   2 When one word ends with a vowel **sound** and the next word begins with a vowel **sound**, we pronounce end consonants which are normally silent.

   /r/
   Where are you?

   /w/
   How old are you?

   /j/
   That's my aunt.

   c Listen and practise saying the sentences above.

   3 Where one word ends in a vowel sound and the next word starts with a vowel sound but there is no consonant, we put an extra one in.

   /r/
   Andrea and Vince

   /w/
   Hello, Andrea.

   /j/
   He isn't here.

   d Try saying the sentences below. What is the linking sound between the words marked?

   I saw a blue and white lorry.
   She isn't very reliable.
   Terry went to Australia and New Zealand.

   e Listen and repeat.

Unit 8
Phonetic alphabet: revision

1 Write this in words.

/wɒt ʃəl wɪ duː tədeɪ/

/lets gəʊ tə ðə biːtʃ/

/ðæts ə gʊd aɪdɪə/ /wɒt əbaʊt meɪkɪŋ ə fɔːsəm wɪð dʒɒn ən ʃærən/

/nəʊ ðeər ɒn hɒlɪdeɪ tɪl θɜːzdeɪ/

Unit 9
Sentence stress

1 a English is a stress-timed language.

1 This means that sentences with the same number of stresses will take the same amount of time regardless of how many syllables they have.

  Example
  Rosy plays the keyboard.
  (three syllables between the stresses)

  Dan plays the drums.
  (two syllables between the stresses)

2 The syllables of words can be made longer or shorter to fit the rhythm.

  What's your name?

  Where are you from?

In the first sentence, there is only one syllable between the two stressed syllables. In the second sentence, there are two. But in each case, they occupy the same time space because in English we reduce the vowels between the main stresses (see Unit 2). In the second sentence **are** is reduced to fit.

b Listen and repeat.

Unit 10
Silent /h/

1 a In fast speech we often don't hear an /h/ sound at the start of a word that isn't stressed.

  Listen to these sentences. Where are the silent /h/ sounds?

  He should have stopped her.

  Has he been to see her?

b Look at these sentences. Where do you think the /h/ will be silent?

  She shouldn't have been driving so fast.

  It wouldn't have happened.

  Vince wouldn't have lost his job.

  Shouldn't he be here?

  Nobody's seen him since.

c Listen and check. Repeat the sentences.

d Look at the words with silent /h/. The /h/ is silent here because the words are not stressed. What sort of words are they?

Unit 11
Strong and weak form prepositions

1 a In Unit 9 we noted that we often reduce syllables between the stresses in a sentence.

Some prepositions have a strong and a weak form. If they are stressed, for example, at the end of questions, they are in the strong form, but if they are in the middle of a sentence and not stressed, they are weak.

Who's your letter from /frɒm/, Vince?
It's from /frəm/ Nottingham University.

b Listen and repeat. Make the stressed prepositions strong, and the ones in the answers weak.

Who were the roses from?
They were from Andrea.

Which university is Sue at?
She's at Oxford.

What did the agent listen to?
He listened to the demo tape.

What was the tape of?
It was of the band.

What was the contract for?
It was for one of the autumn tours.

Unit 12
Phonetic alphabet: revision

1 Write this in words.

/ɪz dɪnə redɪ/

/jes ɪts fɪʃ ən tʃɪps/

/bət wiː hæd ðæt jestədeɪ/

/aɪ nəʊ – aɪ laɪk ɪt/

/səʊ duːw aɪ bət nɒt ðæt mʌtʃ/

/wel ðeər ə səm sɒsɪdʒɪz ɪn ðə frɪdʒ/

/aɪl hæv ðem/

GRAMMAR REFERENCE

1.1 The present simple tense: form

I You We They	like play	football
He She (It)	likes plays	

In the third person singular we add -s to the infinitive.

There are some exceptions. When the verb ends in -ss, -sh, -ch or -o, we add -es.

Examples
miss → misses, wash → washes, catch → catches, go → goes

When the verb ends in -y, we change the -y to -ies.

Example
hurry → hurries

Note also: have → has

To make negatives we use:
subject + don't or doesn't + infinitive.

Examples
I don't live near here.
He doesn't work in a bank.

To make questions we use:
do or does + subject + infinitive.

Examples
'Do you live near here?' 'Yes, I do'.
'Does he work in a bank?' 'No, he doesn't.'

Note: in negatives and questions we use the infinitive ('live', 'work') of the verb. There is no -s on the end in the third person singular.

Examples
She doesn't live here. NOT ~~She doesn't lives here.~~
Does he work here? NOT ~~Does he works here?~~

1.2 The present continuous tense: form

We make the present continuous tense with the verb 'to be' and the -ing form of the verb (the present participle).

Examples
I'm watching TV. She's playing tennis. They're having lunch.
I'm not watching TV. She isn't playing tennis. They aren't having lunch.

For the spelling rules for present participles see Gerunds (3.6) below.

1.3 The present simple tense and the present continuous tense: use

We use the present simple tense to describe regular events or permanent states. We use the present continuous tense to say what is happening at the moment.

Examples
I'm working late today. I usually work late on Wednesdays.
She's singing a song now. She sings well.

Some verbs are not normally used in the continuous form even when they refer to the present moment. They are:
– verbs of liking and disliking: *like, love, prefer, hate, want, wish, need.*
– verbs that describe a mental activity: *think, imagine, believe, know, realize, mean, understand, remember, suppose, feel, hope, see.*
– verbs of appearance: *be, seem, appear, look, sound, taste, smell, feel.*
– verbs that describe a permanent state: *belong to, contain, include, matter, owe, own.*

1.4 Adverbs of frequency

Adverbs of frequency show how often something happens.

Examples
never, seldom, sometimes, often, normally, usually, always

We put the adverb of frequency:
– after the verb 'to be'.
– in front of a normal verb.
– between an auxiliary verb and a main verb.

Examples
She's always late.
I often go to the cinema.
I don't usually forget names.

1.5 The past simple tense: the verb 'to be'

I He She (It)	was was not wasn't	at home here	last week.
We You They	were were not weren't	ill	yesterday.

114

To make questions we put 'was' or 'were' in front of the subject.

>Examples
>'Was she at home?' 'Yes, she was.'
>'Were you on holiday last week?' 'No, I wasn't.'

1.6 The past simple tense: regular verbs

To make the past simple tense we add *-ed* to the infinitive. The past simple is the same for all persons.

>Examples
>**infinitive**   **past simple**
>watch   I watched television last night.
>happen   It happened yesterday.

Spelling exceptions:
When the verb ends in *-e*, we add *-d*.

>Example
>arrive → arrived

When the verb ends in a short vowel and a single consonant, we double the consonant and add *-ed*.

>Example
>stop → stopped

When the verb ends in *-y*, we change the *-y* to *-ied*.

>Example
>carry → carried

1.7 The past simple tense: irregular verbs

Many common verbs have an irregular past form. The irregular form is the same for all persons.

>Examples
>**infinitive**   **past simple**
>come   I came home late.
>go   We went out last night.

See the list of irregular verbs on page 126. Negatives, questions and short answers are the same for all persons and for all verbs except the verb 'to be' (see 1.5 above).
To make negatives we use:
subject + didn't + infinitive

>Example
>I didn't go to the dance.

To make questions we use:
did + subject + infinitive

>Example
>'Did you have a good time?' 'Yes, we did.'

Note: In negatives and questions we use the infinitive form of the verb.

>Example
>*Did you go to the party?* NOT ~~Did you went to the party?~~

2.1 The present perfect tense: form

We make the present perfect tense with the verb 'have/has' and the past participle of the verb.

I You We They	have 've have not haven't	lived in Slovenia. written a book.
He She (It)	has 's has not hasn't	had lunch. been to the USA.

To form regular past participles, we add *-ed* to the infinitive.

>Examples
>work → worked
>play → played

This is the same as the regular past tense. (See 1.6 above for spelling and pronunciation rules.)

Many common verbs have an irregular past participle. See the list of irregular verbs on page 126.

>Examples
>go → gone
>write → written

Note: after words ending in /s/, /z/, /tʃ/, /ʃ/, /dʒ/, we do not normally use the short form of 'has'. We use the full form. In speech this is reduced to /(h)əz/.

To make questions in the present perfect we use:
have/has + subject + past participle

>Examples
>'Have you read this book?' 'Yes, I have.'
>'Has he left yet?' 'No, he hasn't.'

2.2 The present perfect tense: use

The present perfect links the past with the present. We use it in three ways:

– when we are interested in the present result of a past action.

> Examples
> She's gone to the shops. (She's at the shops now.)

– when the activity started in the past and still continues in the present. Note: we do not use the present tense in this context.

> Example
> I've worked here for five years. (And I still work here now.)
> NOT ~~I work here for five years~~. or ~~I am working here for five years~~.

– when we are referring to a time frame that comes up to the present.

> Examples
> I've been to London three times. (Up till now I've been there three times.)
> Have you seen Sue today? (We are still in the time frame of 'today'.)

2.3 The present perfect tense and the past simple tense: use

Compare these uses of the present perfect tense to the past simple tense.

We use the past simple:
– when we are interested in the action or the time of the action not the effect.

> Examples
> She's gone to the shops. (She's at the shops now.)
> She went at ten o'clock. (We're interested in when the action took place.)

– when the action finished in the past.

> Examples
> I've worked here for five years. (I still work here.)
> Before this I worked in a bank. (But I don't work there now.)

– when we are referring to a time frame that ended in the past.

> Example
> 'Have you been out today?' 'Yes, I went out this morning.' NOT ~~I have gone out this morning~~.

Note: when there is a past time reference (e.g. in 1993, two days ago, last week), we must use the past simple tense, not the present perfect.

2.4 The present perfect continuous tense: form and use

I You We They	have 've have not haven't	been	playing football. writing a book.
He She (It)	has 's has not hasn't		waiting for an hour. working in the USA.

To make questions we put 'have' or 'has' in front of the subject.

> Examples
> What have you been doing?
> Have you been waiting long?

We use the present perfect continuous when we want to:
– describe an activity that takes a long time.
– emphasize the length of time that an activity has taken.

> Examples
> 'What have you been doing?' 'I've been painting my room.'
> 'You're late.' 'I've been waiting for an hour.'

With the verbs 'live' and 'work' we can normally use either the present perfect simple or the present perfect continuous.

> Examples
> Have you worked here long?
> Have you been working here long?

2.5 The past continuous tense: form

I He She (It)	was was not wasn't	going to school. having a drink.
We You They	were were not weren't	sitting in the garden.

To make questions we put 'was' or 'were' in front of the subject.

> Examples
> 'Was she talking to John?' 'Yes, she was.'
> 'Were you sitting in the garden?' 'No, we weren't.'

2.6 The past continuous tense: use

The past continuous tense describes a continuous or incomplete activity in the past.

We often use it with the past simple tense. The past continuous sets the scene. The past simple says what happened. The clauses are usually joined by 'while', 'as' or 'when'.

Examples
While he was cooking, the kitchen caught fire.
As we were going to school, we saw Mary.

Compare these two sentences:

While he was cooking, the kitchen caught fire.
When the kitchen caught fire, he ran out of the house.

The first sentence has a past continuous tense to set the scene and a past simple tense to say what happened.

The second sentence has two past simple tenses. One action happened after the other.

2.7 The past perfect tense: form

We make the past perfect tense with 'had/ hadn't' and the past participle.

I He She (It) We You They	had 'd had not hadn't	been here for three years. finished the work. had lunch.

To make questions we use:
had + subject + past participle

Example
How long had they been here?

2.8 The past perfect tense: use

The past perfect describes an event that occurred before another event in the past.

Examples
John went out. Later, Mary arrived.
Mary arrived after John had gone out.

3.1 The future simple tense ('will'): form and use

To make the future simple tense we put 'will' ('ll) in front of the infinitive. To make negatives we use 'will not' (won't).

Examples
I'll be there soon.
We won't stay long.

We use the future with 'will' to make predictions or general statements about the future.

Examples
I won't be here next week.
We'll need some more money.
The weather will be fine.

3.2 First conditionals ('if' clauses 1)

We also use the future simple in first conditionals. First conditionals predict the effects of a real or probable action or event.

Examples
If you're late, we'll miss the plane.
We won't go, if we haven't got any money.

We use the present simple tense in the 'if' clause and the future simple in the main clause.

3.3 'going to': form and use

I	am 'm am not 'm not	going to	watch a video. have dinnner. clean the car. play tennis.
He She (It)	is 's is not isn't		
We You They	are 're are not aren't		

To make questions with 'going to', we put the verb 'to be' in front of the subject.

Examples
What am I going to do?
Are you going to wash up?

'Going to' is the definite future. It means that you have decided to do something or that something will definitely happen.

Examples
Kim's going to buy a car.
It's going to be warm today.

3.4 The present continuous with future meaning

We use the present continuous to talk about arrangements in the future. There is normally a future time expression.

Examples
I'm going away at the weekend.
We're meeting at four o'clock.

3.5 Reduced relative clauses

In a relative clause we can sometimes leave out the relative pronoun.

Examples
That's the guitar that Terry bought.
That's the guitar Terry bought.

We can only do this if the relative pronoun is the object of the clause. So we must say:

This is the shop that sells guitars.

3.6 Gerunds

A gerund is the *-ing* form of a verb. We use it as a noun.
We use gerunds as subjects or objects.

Examples
Skiing is my favourite sport.
I like dancing.

To make gerunds we add *-ing* to the infinitive.

For verbs that end in *-e*, we remove the *-e* and add *-ing*. For verbs with a short vowel and only one consonant, we double the consonant and add *-ing*.

Examples
eat → eating
drive → driving
run → running

5.1 The passive voice: form

We make the passive voice with the verb 'to be' and a past participle.

Example
All our cars are tested.

We can use the passive voice in any tense. To make different tenses we change the verb 'to be'.

Examples:
past: *The car was invented in 1885.*
present perfect: *A new road has been built.*
present: *Millions of new cars are made every year.*
future: *The car will be scrapped.*

To make the negative of the passive voice, we use the negative of the verb 'to be'.

Examples
A sticker wasn't put on the windscreen.
The car hasn't been towed away.
New roads aren't needed.
The tyres won't be recycled.

To make questions, we use the normal question form of the verb 'to be' in each tense.

Examples
Was a sticker put on the windscreen?
Has the car been towed away?
Are new roads needed?
Will the tyres be recycled?

We can use the passive voice with a modal verb. We use this structure
modal verb + be + past participle.

Examples
Cars mustn't be parked here.
Glass can be recycled.

5.2 The passive voice: use

We use the passive voice when the action is more important than who or what did it.

Examples
The car has been tested.
A new road will be built.

If we want to show who or what does the action, we use 'by'.

Examples
The car has been tested by a mechanic.
A new road will be built by the government.

5.3 'used to'

We use 'used to' to talk about things that someone did in the past but doesn't do any longer. It is the same for all subjects.

Examples
I used to live in London. (But I don't now.)
She used to smoke. (But she doesn't now.)

To make questions we use:
did + subject + use to

Examples
Where did you use to live?
Did she use to smoke?

6.1 Question tags: form

When the statement is positive the tag is negative. When the statement is negative the tag is positive.

Examples
You're 17, aren't you?
You aren't 17 yet, are you?

With the verb 'to be' we form the tag with the verb and the subject.

Example
It isn't very warm, is it?

When a verb has an auxiliary, we form the tag from the auxiliary and the subject.

Examples
You can speak French, can't you?
It doesn't matter, does it?
You've been to Lisbon, haven't you?

When the verb hasn't got an auxiliary, we form the tag from the auxiliary that we would normally use for making questions in that tense.

Examples
He left yesterday, didn't he?
You like heavy metal, don't you?

When the subject of the statement is a noun, we replace it with a pronoun in the tag.

Examples
Andrea's from Argentina, isn't she?
Dan and Rosy are students, aren't they?

When we write a question tag it is separated from the statement by a comma (,) and is followed by a question mark (?).

6.2 Question tags: use

A question tag turns a statement into a question. We usually use a question tag when we are fairly sure of the answer. It is less direct than an ordinary question.

We can use a falling intonation or rising intonation on the tag. Falling intonation means that we expect the person to agree with the statement. Rising intonation is less certain. We use it to check something.

6.3 (not) want someone to …

When someone wants (or doesn't want) another person to do something, we use this structure:
want + object + to + verb

Examples
We wanted them to stay.
Vince didn't want Kim to leave.

6.4 Numbers

We say decimal numbers like this:
2.75: two point seven five

To make fractions we use ordinal numbers.

Example
2/3: two thirds, 1/10: one tenth

We say percentages like this:
80%: eighty per cent

After percentages and fractions we use 'of' except after 'half'.

Examples
two-thirds of the population; sixty per cent of the country
But: half the people

In large numbers we put 'and' before any number less than a hundred.

Words like 'billion', 'million', 'thousand' and 'hundred' are always singular.

In figures we separate hundreds, thousands and millions with commas.

Examples
345: three hundred and forty-five
8,050: eight thousand and fifty
670,000,000: six hundred and seventy million

6.5 Second conditionals ('if' clauses 2)

In second conditionals we use the conditional form ('would') in the main clause and the past tense in the 'if' clause. Note: we do not use 'would' in the 'if' clause.

Example
If we had more money, we'd buy a new car.
NOT ~~If we would have more money, we'd buy a car.~~

Second conditionals describe unreal, unlikely or imaginary situations.

Examples
What would you do if you won the lottery?
If I went to another planet, I'd miss my friends.

7.1 Reported speech

In reported speech we report what somebody says. The pronouns and possessive adjectives change, because a different person is now speaking. We normally introduce reported speech with 'that'.

Examples
direct speech: *(Terry is talking) I like travelling.*
reported speech: *(Kim is talking) Terry says that he likes travelling.*

When we report something with a past tense verb ('said' or 'told'), some of the tenses of the verbs also change.

direct speech	→ reported speech
present perfect	→ past perfect
past simple	→ past perfect
present simple	→ past simple
present continuous	→ past continuous
future simple	→ conditional

The past perfect and the conditional tenses do not change.

Examples

Direct speech	Reported speech
Frank: I've seen that film.	Frank said that he had seen that film.
June: We had a great holiday.	June said that they had had a great holiday.
Barry: I don't feel well.	Barry said that he didn't feel well.
Kate: I'm going away.	Kate said that she was going away.
Dan: I'll be there by six.	Dan said that he would be there by six.
Rosy: I would like a pizza.	Rosy said that she would like a pizza.
Peter: I had never been there before.	Peter said that he had never been there before.

7.2 'say' and 'tell'

We 'say' something. We 'tell' somebody.

Examples
Kim said (that) she was going away.
Kim told Rosy (that) she was going away.

7.3 Reported speech questions

When we report questions, we make the following changes:
– the tenses and pronouns change as for statements.
– the word order changes to a statement word order.
– verbs have a statement form.

There is no question mark at the end of a reported question.

With 'yes/no' questions, the reported question starts with 'whether' or 'if'.

Examples
'Where does Kim work?' Andrea asked Vince where Kim worked.
'Have you seen Kim?' Dan asked Rosy whether she had seen Kim.

7.4 Reported speech: commands and requests

To report a command or a request we use the following structure. We use 'tell' for commands and 'ask' for requests:
told/asked + person + (not) to + verb

If the person is a pronoun we use an object pronoun ('me', 'him/her', 'it', 'us', 'you', 'them').

Examples
'Be careful.' Sir Walter told Digby to be careful.
'Please look after Isabel.' He asked him to look after Isabel.
'Don't tell Spencer anything.' He told them not to tell Spencer anything.

7.5 Reflexive pronouns

These are the reflexive pronouns:

singular	plural
myself	ourselves
yourself	yourselves
himself	themselves
herself	
itself	

We use reflexive pronouns in two ways.
– when the object is the same as the subject.
– for emphasis.

Examples
We don't go to the movies to see ourselves.
And do you like these superhero films yourself?

7.6 Agreeing and disagreeing

To agree with a positive statement we use:
So + auxiliary verb + subject.

To agree with a negative statement we use:
Nor + auxiliary verb + subject.

To disagree with a positive statement we use:
Oh, I + negative auxiliary verb.

To disagree with a negative statement we use:
Oh, I + positive auxiliary verb.

With the verb 'to be' or if the verb already has an auxiliary, we use that.

If the verb hasn't got an auxiliary, we use the auxiliary that we would normally use for a question in that tense.

Examples
'He's from London.' 'So am I.' 'Oh, I'm not.'
'I haven't bought any records lately.' 'Nor have I.' 'Oh, I have.'
'I like spaghetti.' 'So do I.' 'Oh, I don't.'

9.1 Present participles

Present participles (*-ing* forms) are used in several different ways.
– to describe what is (or was) happening.

Examples
There's someone coming.
There were two people crossing the road.

– to describe what someone can sense ('see', 'hear', 'feel', 'watch', 'smell', 'notice', etc.).

Examples
I heard someone crying.
We saw two people playing tennis.
I can smell something burning.

– with 'start', 'stop' and 'continue'.

Examples
They have stopped smoking.
The band has already started playing.
They continued arguing for hours.

– to describe how something is done.

Example
She changed her hair by dyeing it.

– to say what you want.

Example
He wants his car cleaning.

9.2 Participles as adjectives

The participles of some verbs can be used as adjectives. We can use both the present participle and the past participle but they have different meanings.

present participle	past participle
boring	bored
interesting	interested
exciting	excited
amazing	amazed

The present participle has an active meaning. The past participle has a passive meaning.

Examples
He is amazing. (He amazes people.)
He is amazed. (Something is amazing him.)

10.1 'should/shouldn't have'

If we want to express regret, we use:
should/shouldn't + have + past participle

Examples
Terry shouldn't have told Vince about the agent.
He should have waited till later.

The structure is the same for all persons.

I He She (It) We You They	should shouldn't	have	gone away. told him. got up late.

We can also use this structure in the continuous form:
should/shouldn't + have been + present participle

Examples
Kim shouldn't have been driving so fast.
She should have been paying more attention.

10.2 Unfulfilled conditions ('if' clauses 3)

When we want to express regret we can talk about a condition that didn't actually happen. This is called an unfulfilled condition. We use the following structure:
If + past perfect (continuous) + conditional perfect
or
conditional perfect + if + past perfect (continuous).

Examples
If Vince had told the truth, Kim wouldn't have been so angry.
If Kim hadn't been driving so fast, she wouldn't have had an accident.
or
Kim wouldn't have been so angry if Vince had told the truth.
Kim wouldn't have had an accident if she hadn't been driving so fast.

The conditional perfect is the same for all persons.

I He She (It) We You They	would wouldn't	have	had an accident. been sick. got the sack.

10.3 have something done

If we want to show that a job was done by someone else, we use:
have + object + past participle

Examples
I painted my room.
(This means that the room was painted and I did it myself.)
I had my room painted.
(This means that the room was painted but I didn't do it myself. Someone else did it for me.)

10.4 'make'/'get'/'let'

'Make', 'get' and 'let' show that one person has influenced another person's behaviour. 'Make' and 'let' are followed by a simple infinitive. 'Get' is followed by an infinitive with 'to'.

'Make' means that one person forces another person to do something that they probably don't want to do.

Example
The judge made the man pay a fine.

'Get to' means that one person persuades (or asks) another person to do something.

Example
The men got the assistant to hold the door open.

'Let' means that one person allows another person to do something.

Example
John's father lets him drive the car.

10.5 'to hospital/to the hospital'

We can use the names of places, such as prison, hospital, school, church, university, court, without a definite article ('the') or with a definite article. But the meaning is different.

When you mean the function of the place, there is no article.

Examples
You go to hospital when you are ill.
The bank robbers are in prison now.

When you mean the building, there is an article.

Examples
We went to the hospital to visit our friends.
There was a fire in the prison.

11.1 Direct and indirect objects

In the example sentence below the direct object shows us what was sent. The indirect object shows us who it was sent to.

Example

subject	verb	direct object	indirect object
The agent	sent	a contract	to Rosy.

We can show an indirect object in two ways:
– we put 'to' in front of the indirect object and put it after the direct object.
– we put the indirect object in front of the direct object without 'to'. We normally don't do this when the direct object is a pronoun.

Examples
Rosy wrote a letter to the agent.
But she didn't send it to him straightaway.
First she showed it to the others.
She showed the letter to them on Saturday.

Rosy wrote the agent a letter.
But she didn't send him it straightaway.
(First she showed the others it.)
She showed them the letter on Saturday.

11.2 Passive with an indirect subject

When there is both an indirect and a direct object, it is normally the indirect object that becomes the subject of a passive sentence, like this.

Example
Active: *The shop offered John a job.*
Passive: *John was offered a job by the shop.*
NOT ~~A job was offered to John by the shop.~~

11.3 'one/ones'

'One' is used to replace a noun. We usually do this so that we don't have to repeat a noun, or if it is obvious from the context what we are referring to.

We use 'ones' to replace a plural noun.

Examples
'Which is your car?' 'It's the blue one.'
'Do you like these shoes?' 'I prefer the ones over there.'

WORDLIST

INTRODUCTION

academy /ə'kædəmɪ/
accept /ək'sept/
any day now /ˌenɪ deɪ 'naʊ/
ask for /'ɑːsk fə(r), fɔː(r)/
at the end of /ət ði 'end əv/
be surprised /bɪ sə'praɪzd/
corridor /'kɒrɪdɔː(r)/
good luck /ˌgʊd 'lʌk/
interview (v.) /'ɪntəvjuː/
late for work /ˌleɪt fə 'wɜːk/
luggage /'lʌgɪdʒ/
practise /'præktɪs/
sports stuff /'spɔːtstʌf/
straight /streɪt/
take a year out /ˌteɪk ə jɪər 'aʊt/
tennis racquet /'tenɪs ˌrækɪt/
trainers /'treɪnəz/
trolley /'trɒlɪ/
turn up /ˌtɜːn 'ʌp/

UNIT 1 WHO ARE YOU?

alcohol /'ælkəhɒl/
amaze /ə'meɪz/
ambitious /æm'bɪʃəs/
anxious /'æŋkʃəs/
anyway /'enɪweɪ/
awake /ə'weɪk/
backwards /'bækwədz/
basket /'bɑːskɪt/
bass guitar /ˌbeɪs gɪ'tɑː(r)/
behaviour /bɪ'heɪvjə(r)/
champion /'tʃæmpɪən/
chime (v.) /tʃaɪm/
church hall /ˌtʃɜːtʃ 'hɔːl/
confident /'kɒnfɪdənt/
control (v.) /kən'trəʊl/
court /kɔːt/
crowds /kraʊdz/
curled up /ˌkɜːld 'ʌp/
defensive /dɪ'fensɪv/
degree /dɪ'griː/
depressed /dɪ'prest/
drummer /'drʌmə(r)/
education /edjʊ'keɪʃən/
every single day /ˌevrɪ ˌsɪŋgl 'deɪ/
fall in love /ˌfɔːl ɪn 'lʌv/
fortunately /'fɔːtʃənətlɪ/
frequently /'friːkwəntlɪ/
gear /gɪə(r)/
get into trouble /get ɪntuː 'trʌbl/
goal /gəʊl/
gonna (slang: going to) /'gɒnə/
grab /græb/
grow up /ˌgrəʊ 'ʌp/
hairdresser's /'heədresəz/
have a low opinion of /ˌhæv ə ləʊ ə'pɪnjən əv/
head (v.) /hed/
jump /dʒʌmp/
keyboard(s) /'kiːbɔːd(z)/
late /leɪt/
lead (v.) /liːd/
lead guitar /ˌliːd gɪ'tɑː(r)/
medal /'medəl/
mend /mend/
mike (slang) /maɪk/
mind (n.) /maɪnd/
natural /'nætʃrəl/
nervous /'nɜːvəs/
normally /'nɔːməlɪ/
number /'nʌmbə(r)/
on (my / your etc) back /ɒn ...'bæk/
on (my / your etc) side /ɒn ...'saɪd/
on (my / your etc) stomach /ɒn ...'stʌmək/
open (adj.) /'əʊpn/
opponent /ə'pəʊnənt/
perfect /'pɜːfekt/
point /pɔɪnt/
position /pə'zɪʃn/
professional /prə'feʃnl/
race /reɪs/
relationship /rɪ'leɪʃnʃɪp/
rhythm guitar /ˌrɪðm gɪ'tɑː(r)/
sarcastic /sɑː'kæstɪk/
secretive /'siːkrətɪv/
shuffle (my / your etc) feet /ʃʌfl ...'fiːt/
shy /ʃaɪ/
skill /skɪl/
slam /slæm/
slow down /ˌsləʊ 'daʊn/
snap (my / your etc) fingers /ˌsnæp ...'fɪŋgəz/
stand in (for) /stænd 'ɪn fə(r), fɔː(r)/
stay away from /steɪ ə'weɪ frɒm/
still /stɪl/
straight /streɪt/
strength /streŋθ/
stubborn /'stʌbn/
upset (v.) /ʌp'set/
voice /vɔɪs/
weakness /'wiːknəs/
wedding bells /'wedɪŋ belz/

UNIT 2 TRAVELLERS

a couple of /ə 'kʌpl əv/
a long time /ə ˌlɒŋ 'taɪm/
alive /ə'laɪv/
Antarctica /æn'tɑːktɪkə/
base /beɪs/
be around /bɪ ə'raʊnd/
beat ... to it /biːt ... 'tuː ɪt/
bet /bet/
bitterly /'bɪtəlɪ/
break down /ˌbreɪk 'daʊn/
Cape Horn /ˌkeɪp 'hɔːn/
choose /tʃuːz/
companion /kəm'pænɪən/
cross (v.) /krɒs/
disappear /dɪsə'pɪə(r)/
disappointed /dɪsə'pɔɪntɪd/
dull /dʌl/
enjoy /ɪn'dʒɔɪ/
expedition /ekspə'dɪʃn/
explorer /ɪk'splɔːrə(r)/
fault /fɒlt/
forget /fə'get/
fuel /fjʊəl/
(get) seasick /'siːsɪk/
guitarist /gɪ'tɑːrɪst/
hero /'hɪərəʊ/
ice /aɪs/
It seems like it /ɪt 'siːmz laɪk ɪt/
lie (v.) /laɪ/
lucky /'lʌkɪ/
lunch break /'lʌntʃ breɪk/
mostly /'məʊstlɪ/
motor sledge /'məʊtə sledʒ/
New Zealand /njuː 'ziːlənd/
Norwegian /nɔː'wiːdʒən/
on board /ɒn 'bɔːd/
originally /ə'rɪdʒənəlɪ/
place (v.) /pleɪs/
plan (v.) /plæn/
practice session /'præktɪs ˌseʃn/
reach /riːtʃ/
rival /'raɪvəl/
route /ruːt/
run into /rʌn 'ɪntuː, 'ɪntə/
sail (v.) /seɪl/
serious /'sɪərɪəs/
set off /set 'ɒf/
shock /ʃɒk/
sledge /sledʒ/
snowstorm /'snəʊstɔːm/
somehow /'sʌmhaʊ/
step (v.) /step/
well-balanced /ˌwel 'bælənst/
Would you mind ...ing? /'wʊd juː ˌmaɪnd/
suppose /sə'pəʊz/
survive /sə'vaɪv/
terrible /'terəbl/
That sounds ... /ðæt saʊndz/
the North Pole /ðə ˌnɔːθ 'pəʊl/
the rest of /ðə 'rest əv/
the South Pole /ðə ˌsaʊθ 'pəʊl/
Things have a habit of going wrong. /'θɪŋz hæv ə ˌhæbɪt əv ˌgəʊɪŋ 'rɒŋ/
trap (v.) /træp/
trip /trɪp/

UNIT 3 AMBITIONS

a handful /ə 'hændfʊl/
a must (slang) /ə 'mʌst/
a set of wheels (slang) /ə ˌset əv 'wiːlz/
a waste of money /ə ˌweɪst əv 'mʌnɪ/
acoustic guitar /əˌkuːstɪk gɪ'tɑː(r)/
afford /ə'fɔːd/
amplifier /'æmplɪˌfaɪə(r)/
arrange /ə'reɪndʒ/
audience /'ɔːdɪəns/
avoid /ə'vɔɪd/
be into sth (slang) /bɪ 'ɪntə/
break up /ˌbreɪk 'ʌp/
career /kə'rɪə(r)/
chambermaid /'tʃeɪmbəmeɪd/
case /keɪs/
certainly /'sɜːtənlɪ/
constantly /'kɒnstəntlɪ/
contract (n.) /'kɒntrækt/
deal with /'diːl wɪð/
decent (slang: good) /'diːsənt/
dirty /'dɜːtɪ/
discount (n.) /'dɪskaʊnt/
drumsticks /'drʌmstɪks/
equipment /ɪ'kwɪpmənt/
factory /'fæktərɪ/
fond of /'fɒnd əv/
get changed /get 'tʃeɪndʒd/
get knocked over /ˌget ˌnɒkt 'əʊvə(r)/
get on well /get ɒn 'wel/
gig (slang) /gɪg/
go up in smoke /ˌgəʊ ˌʌp ɪn 'sməʊk/
good quality (adj.) /ˌgʊd 'kwɒlətɪ/
handle (v.) /'hændl/

hit the big time /ˌhɪt ðə ˈbɪg ˌtaɪm/
loudspeaker /ˌlaʊdˈspiːkə(r)/
nick (v., slang) /nɪk/
offer (v.) /ˈɒfə(r)/
performance /pəˈfɔːməns/
radiator /ˈreɪdɪeɪtə(r)/
reception desk /rɪˈsepʃn desk/
recording agent /rɪˈkɔːdɪŋ ˌeɪdʒənt/
relax /rɪˈlæks/
romance /ˈrəʊmæns/
sceptical /ˈskeptɪkl/
serve /sɜːv/
shelf /ʃelf/
shop assistant /ˈʃɒp əˌsɪstənt/
smart /smɑːt/
smile /smaɪl/
stadium /ˈsteɪdɪəm/
sweep /swiːp/
unpack /ʌnˈpæk/
work experience /ˈwɜːk ɪkˌspɪərɪəns/
workplace /ˈwɜːkpleɪs/

UNIT 4 REVISION

a dirty joke /ə ˌdɜːtɪ ˈdʒəʊk/
advice /ədˈvaɪs/
alcohol /ˈælkəhɒl/
argue /ˈɑːgjuː/
caller /ˈkɔːlə(r)/
can't stand sth /kɑːnt ˈstænd/
cardboard box /ˌkɑːdbɔːd ˈbɒks/
Christmas tree /ˈkrɪsməs ˌtriː/
cigarette /sɪgəˈret/
concern (n.) /kənˈsɜːn/
decorate /ˈdekəreɪt/
drugs /drʌgz/
either /ˈaɪðə(r)/
exam /ɪgˈzæm/
get on with /ˈget ɒn wɪð/
grow up /ˌgrəʊ ˈʌp/
I didn't see the point of... /aɪ ˌdɪdnt siː ðə ˈpɔɪnt əv/
on the line /ɒn ðə ˈlaɪn/
pavement /ˈpeɪvmənt/
phone-in /ˈfəʊnɪn/
rights /raɪts/
run away /ˌrʌn əˈweɪ/
subject (n.) /ˈsʌbdʒekt/
survey /ˈsɜːveɪ/
untidy /ˌʌnˈtaɪdɪ/
worry (n.) /ˈwʌrɪ/

UNIT 5 MOTOR MANIA

a used car /ə ˌjuːzd ˈkɑː(r)/
accelerate /əkˈseləreɪt/
acid rain /ˌæsɪd ˈreɪn/
assembly line /əˈsemblɪ ˌlaɪn/
at once /ət ˈwʌns/
automobile (adj.) /ˈɔːtəməbiːl/
battery /ˈbætərɪ/
bend (n.) /bend/
bonnet /ˈbɒnɪt/
boot /buːt/
bottle bank /ˈbɒtl bæŋk/
bribe (n.) /braɪb/
bribery /ˈbraɪbərɪ/
bunch /bʌntʃ/
bury /ˈberɪ/
cable /ˈkeɪbl/
call sb names /ˌkɔːl ...ˈneɪmz/
(car) pound /paʊnd/
carbon monoxide /ˌkɑːbən mɒˈnɒksaɪd/
cave /keɪv/
crossing /ˈkrɒsɪŋ/
crush /krʌʃ/
darling /ˈdɑːlɪŋ/
dashboard /ˈdæʃbɔːd/
Do you fancy ...? /djuː ˈfænsɪ .../
double-park /ˌdʌbl ˈpɑːk/
embrace (n.) /ɪmˈbreɪs/
emergency /ɪˈmɜːdʒənsɪ/
environment /ɪnˈvaɪərənmənt/
fire engine /ˈfaɪər ˌendʒɪn/
freedom /ˈfriːdəm/
global /ˈgləʊbl/
go for a spin /ˌgəʊ fər ə ˈspɪn/
greenhouse gases /ˈgriːnhaʊs ˌgæsɪz/
Happy Anniversary /ˌhæpɪ ænɪˈvɜːsərɪ/
heat (v.) /hiːt/
highway /ˈhaɪweɪ/
illegally /ɪˈliːgəlɪ/
internal combustion engine /ɪnˌtɜːnl kəmˈbʌstʃən ˌendʒɪn/
label /ˈleɪbl/
last wish /ˌlɑːst ˈwɪʃ/
lecture (n.) /ˈlektʃə(r)/
lorry /ˈlɒrɪ/
make a foursome /ˌmeɪk ə ˈfɔːsəm/

manage without /ˈmænɪdʒ wɪˌðaʊt/
mixture /ˈmɪkstʃə(r)/
motor /ˈməʊtə(r)/
motorist /ˈməʊtərɪst/
off the ground /ˌɒf ðə ˈgraʊnd/
oil /ɔɪl/
paintwork /ˈpeɪntwɜːk/
persuade /pəˈsweɪd/
poacher /ˈpəʊtʃə(r)/
polish (v.) /ˈpɒlɪʃ/
pollute /pəˈluːt/
pollution /pəˈluːʃn/
power station /ˈpaʊə ˌsteɪʃn/
pregnant /ˈpregnənt/
price /praɪs/
progress (n.) /ˈprəʊgres/
pump into /ˈpʌmp ɪntə/
put (sth) down /ˌpʊt ...ˈdaʊn/
recycle /riːˈsaɪkl/
recycling plant /riːˈsaɪklɪŋ plɑːnt/
remove /rɪˈmuːv/
respray /ˌriːˈspreɪ/
road test /ˈrəʊd test/
scrap (v.) /skræp/
scream (v.) /skriːm/
shout (at) /ʃaʊt (ət, æt)/
smallpox /ˈsmɔːlpɒks/
smart /smɑːt/
sob story /ˈsɒb ˌstɔːrɪ/
steering wheel /ˈstɪərɪŋ wiːl/
sticker /ˈstɪkə(r)/
Stonehenge /ˌstəʊnˈhendʒ/
streak of lightning /ˌstriːk əv ˈlaɪtnɪŋ/
swear (at) /sweə(r) (ət, æt)/
thorough(ly) /ˈθʌrə(lɪ)/
threat /θret/
thunder /ˈθʌndə(r)/
top /tɒp/
tow away /ˌtəʊ əˈweɪ/
tow-away team /ˈtəʊ əweɪ ˌtiːm/
toxic /ˈtɒksɪk/
traffic jam /ˈtræfɪk dʒæm/
traffic warden /ˈtræfɪk ˌwɔːdn/
tyre /ˈtaɪə(r)/
unpopular /ˌʌnˈpɒpjʊlə(r)/
valve /vælv/
waste (my/your etc.) time /ˌweɪst ...ˈtaɪm/
wasteful /ˈweɪstfl/
whatever /wɒˈtevə(r)/
wind /wɪnd/

worldwide /ˌwɜːldˈwaɪd/
worn /wɔːn/

UNIT 6 FARAWAY PLACES

Aborigine /ˌæbəˈrɪdʒənɪ/
ammunition /ˌæmjʊˈnɪʃn/
ant /ænt/
area /ˈeərɪə/
Asian /ˈeɪʃn/
aspect /ˈæspekt/
astronaut /ˈæstrənɔːt/
biscuit /ˈbɪskɪt/
blanket /ˈblæŋkɪt/
box of matches /ˌbɒks əv ˈmætʃɪz/
century /ˈsentʃərɪ/
climate /ˈklaɪmɪt/
coin /kɔɪn/
Commonwealth /ˈkɒmənwelθ/
compass /ˈkʌmpəs/
convict (n.) /ˈkɒnvɪkt/
currency /ˈkʌrənsɪ/
distance /ˈdɪstəns/
enormous /ɪˈnɔːməs/
fall over /ˌfɔːl ˈəʊvə(r)/
feature /ˈfiːtʃə(r)/
federal /ˈfedrəl/
first aid /ˌfɜːst ˈeɪd/
first aid kit /fɜːst ˈeɪd ˌkɪt/
get a cold /ˌget ə ˈkəʊld/
have fun /ˌhæv ˈfʌn/
hay fever /ˈheɪ ˌfiːvə(r)/
Head of Government /ˌhed əv ˈgʌvənmənt/
Head of State /ˌhed əv ˈsteɪt/
hitch a lift /ˌhɪtʃ ə ˈlɪft/
inflatable /ɪnˈfleɪtəbl/
in orbit /ɪn ˈɔːbɪt/
It must be nice to ... /ɪt ˌmʌst bɪ ˈnaɪs tə/
kangaroo /ˌkæŋgəˈruː/
koala /kəʊˈɑːlə/
lifetime /ˈlaɪftaɪm/
light year /ˈlaɪt jɪə(r)/
litre /ˈliːtə(r)/
mining /ˈmaɪnɪŋ/
mirror /ˈmɪrə(r)/
monarch /ˈmɒnək/
mysterious /mɪˈstɪərɪəs/
official /əˈfɪʃl/
opera house /ˈɒprə ˌhaʊs/
origin /ˈɒrɪdʒɪn/
(pair of) binoculars /(ˌpeər əv) bɪˈnɒkjʊləz/
picnic /ˈpɪknɪk/
planet /ˈplænɪt/

platypus /ˈplætɪpəs/
political structure /pəˌlɪtɪkl ˈstrʌktʃə(r)/
relation /rɪˈleɪʃn/
rocket /ˈrɒkɪt/
rope /rəʊp/
semi- /ˈsemi/
settler /ˈsetlə(r)/
sleeping bag /ˈsliːpɪŋ ˌbæg/
solar system /ˈsəʊlə ˌsɪstəm/
source of income /ˌsɔːs əv ˈɪŋkʌm/
spaceship /ˈspeɪsʃɪp/
spare /speə(r)/
speed /spiːd/
spot (n.) /spɒt/
square kilometre /skweə ˈkɪləmiːtə(r), kɪˈlɒmɪtə(r)/
star /stɑː(r)/
stretcher /ˈstretʃə(r)/
sunny /ˈsʌni/
temperate /ˈtempərət/
the Great Barrier Reef /ðə ˌgreɪt ˌbæriə ˈriːf/
tissue /ˈtɪʃuː/
toothbrush /ˈtuːθbrʌʃ/
toothpaste /ˈtuːθpeɪst/
torch /tɔːtʃ/
transport (v.) /trænsˈpɔːt/
travel /ˈtrævl/
Walkman /ˈwɔːkmən/
wide, open spaces /ˌwaɪd ˌəʊpn ˈspeɪsɪz/

UNIT 7 CONFLICT

adventure film /ədˈventʃə fɪlm/
airfield /ˈeəfiːld/
archaeologist /ˌɑːkiˈɒlədʒɪst/
as if /əz ˈɪf/
barrel /ˈbærəl/
be in touch with /biː ɪn ˈtʌtʃ wɪð/
big business /ˌbɪg ˈbɪznɪs/
chamber /ˈtʃeɪmbə(r)/
cheetah /ˈtʃiːtə/
comic book /ˈkɒmɪk bʊk/
conflict (n.) /ˈkɒnflɪkt/
diamond /ˈdaɪəmənd/
doorway /ˈdɔːweɪ/
emerald /ˈemərəld/
entrance /ˈentrəns/
event /ɪˈvent/
evil /ˈiːvl/
fabulous(ly) /ˈfæbjʊləsli/
film critic /ˈfɪlm ˌkrɪtɪk/
gentle /ˈdʒentl/
good-looking /ˌgʊd ˈlʊkɪŋ/

guard (v.) /gɑːd/
head (v.) for /ˈhed fə(r)/
incredible /ɪnˈkredɪbl/
legend /ˈledʒənd/
long ago /ˌlɒŋ əˈgəʊ/
love life /ˈlʌv laɪf/
make (my/your etc) mind /meɪk ʌp … ˈmaɪnd/
moral /ˈmɒrəl/
on the edge of /ɒn ði ˈedʒ əv/
place (v.) /pleɪs/
pretty (adv., slang) /ˈprɪti/
profit /ˈprɒfɪt/
properly /ˈprɒpəli/
real-life (adj.) /rɪəl laɪf/
reason /ˈriːzn/
roar into life /ˌrɔːr ˌɪntə ˈlaɪf/
rough /rʌf/
ruby /ˈruːbi/
runway /ˈrʌnweɪ/
sapphire /ˈsæfaɪə(r)/
science fiction /ˌsaɪəns ˈfɪkʃn/
servant /ˈsɜːvənt/
special effect /ˌspeʃl ɪˈfekt/
spectacular /ˌspekˈtækjʊlə(r)/
standards (n.) /ˈstændədz/
step (n.) /step/
stunt /stʌnt/
sulk (v.) /sʌlk/
swerve /swɜːv/
the good guys /ðə ˈgʊd ˌgaɪz/
tough /tʌf/
treasure /ˈtreʒə(r)/
truthful(ly) /ˈtruːθfʊl(i)/
turn over /ˌtɜːn ˈəʊvə(r)/
unfair /ˌʌnˈfeə(r)/
villain /ˈvɪlən/
What the heck …? /wɒt ðə ˈhek …/
wish sb luck /ˌwɪʃ … ˈlʌk/

UNIT 8 REVISION

approach /əˈprəʊtʃ/
bird cage /ˈbɜːd keɪdʒ/
budgerigar /ˈbʌdʒərɪˌgɑː(r)/
budgie /ˈbʌdʒi/
calmly /ˈkɑːmli/
difference /ˈdɪfrəns/
doorbell /ˈdɔːbel/
freeze /friːz/
gas /gæs/
horror /ˈhɒrə(r)/
in a cold sweat /ɪn ə ˌkəʊld ˈswet/
lift (n.) /lɪft/

light (v.) /laɪt/
motorbike /ˈməʊtəˌbaɪk/
notice (v.) /ˈnəʊtɪs/
pet shop /ˈpet ʃɒp/
pillion /ˈpɪliən/
pull off the road /ˌpʊl ɒf ðə ˈrəʊd/
turn off /ˌtɜːn ˈɒf/
turn on /ˌtɜːn ˈɒn/

UNIT 9 IMAGE

action /ˈækʃn/
advert /ˈædvɜːt/
advise /ədˈvaɪz/
aim /eɪm/
anonymity /ˌænəˈnɪməti/
anonymous /əˈnɒnɪməs/
authority /ɔːˈθɒrəti/
bald /bɔːld/
be associated with /bɪ əˈsəʊsieɪtɪd wɪð/
bleach (v.) /bliːtʃ/
bun /bʌn/
business executive /ˌbɪznɪs ɪgˈzekjʊtɪv/
calmness /ˈkɑːmnəs/
clipper /ˈklɪpə(r)/
conditioner /kənˈdɪʃənə(r)/
consultant /kənˈsʌltənt/
cosmetics /kɒzˈmetɪks/
coward /ˈkaʊəd/
create /kriˈeɪt/
curl (v.) /kɜːl/
discuss /dɪsˈkʌs/
dreadlocks /ˈdredlɒks/
effect /ɪˈfekt/
energy /ˈenədʒi/
excitement /ɪkˈsaɪtmənt/
fire (v.) sb /ˈfaɪə(r)/
flag /flæg/
follicle /ˈfɒlɪkl/
freedom /ˈfriːdəm/
friendliness /ˈfrendlinəs/
gangster /ˈgæŋstə(r)/
gel /dʒel/
grease /griːs/
group identity /ˌgruːp aɪˈdentəti/
hairdryer /ˈheəˌdraɪə(r)/
hairspray /ˈheəspreɪ/
half an inch /ˌhɑːf ən ˈɪntʃ/
I might have known. /aɪ ˌmaɪt əv ˈnəʊn/
image /ˈɪmɪdʒ/
keep out of /kiːp ˈaʊt əv/
layer (v.) /ˈleɪə(r)/
left wing /ˌleft ˈwɪŋ/
logo /ˈləʊgəʊ/
monk /mʌŋk/
mousse /muːs/

obviously /ˈɒbviəsli/
openness /ˈəʊpənnes/
part (v.) /pɑːt/
peace /piːs/
perm (v.) /pɜːm/
plait (v.) /plæt/
power /ˈpaʊə(r)/
produce /prəˈdjuːs/
producer /prəˈdjuːsə(r)/
punk /pʌŋk/
purity /ˈpjʊərəti/
rasta /ˈræstə/
razor /ˈreɪzə(r)/
relaxation /ˌriːlækˈseɪʃn/
relaxing /rɪˈlæksɪŋ/
ribbon /ˈrɪbn/
roller-skate (v.) /ˈrəʊləˌskeɪt/
Samurai /ˈsæmərai/
sensitive to /ˈsensətɪv tə, tuː/
serve (v.) /sɜːv/
shave off /ˌʃeɪv ˈɒf/
skinhead /ˈskɪnhed/
slide (n.) /slaɪd/
sort out /ˌsɔːt ˈaʊt/
spike /spaɪk/
stimulate /ˈstɪmjʊleɪt/
straighten /ˈstreɪtn/
strength /streŋθ/
stubble /ˈstʌbl/
successful /səkˈsesfʊl/
talk things over /ˌtɔːk θɪŋz ˈəʊvə(r)/
thin (v.) out /ˌθɪn ˈaʊt/
threatening /ˈθretnɪŋ/
tiring /ˈtaɪərɪŋ/
trim (n.) /trɪm/
vampire /ˈvæmpaɪə(r)/
versatile /ˈvɜːsətaɪl/
warmth /wɔːmθ/
warrior /ˈwɒriə(r)/
wig /wɪg/

UNIT 10 MISTAKES

a happy ending /ə ˌhæpi ˈendɪŋ/
admit /ədˈmɪt/
bank robber /ˈbæŋk ˌrɒbə(r)/
blame (v.) /bleɪm/
branch /brɑːntʃ/
break up with /ˌbreɪk ˈʌp wɪð/
burglar /ˈbɜːglə(r)/
character /ˈkærəktə(r)/
clear (v.) /klɪə(r)/
collection note /kəˈlekʃn ˌnəʊt/
come true /ˌkʌm ˈtruː/

comfort (v.) /ˈkʌmfət/
concern (n.) /kənˈsɜːn/
department store /dɪˈpɑːtmənt ˌstɔː(r)/
driving test /ˈdraɪvɪŋ test/
entrance exam /ˈentrəns ɪɡˌzæm/
general /ˈdʒenrəl/
get the sack /ˌget ðə ˈsæk/
go mad /ˌɡəʊ ˈmæd/
haunt /hɔːnt/
have it rough /ˌhæv ɪt ˈrʌf/
in the dock /ɪn ðə ˈdɒk/
joke /dʒəʊk/
keep (my, your etc) fingers crossed /ˌkiːp ... ˈfɪŋɡəz krɒst/
literature /ˈlɪtrətʃə(r)/
murder /ˈmɜːdə(r)/
nothing serious /ˌnʌθɪŋ ˈsɪərɪəs/
opening scene /ˈəʊpnɪŋ ˌsiːn/
overalls /ˈəʊvərɔːlz/
pay a fine /peɪ ə ˈfaɪn/
pompous /ˈpɒmpəs/
prophecy /ˈprɒfəsɪ/
put (my/your etc) foot in it /ˌpʊt ...ˈfʊt ɪn ɪt/
put sth into reverse /ˌpʊt ... ɪntə rɪˈvɜːs/
revenge /rɪˈvendʒ/
robbery /ˈrɒbərɪ/
roll up /ˌrəʊl ˈʌp/
rotten /ˈrɒtn/
send to prison /ˌsend tə ˈprɪzn/
siren /ˈsaɪərən/
state /steɪt/
step on /ˈstep ɒn/
stink bomb /ˈstɪŋk bɒm/
storm off /ˌstɔːm ˈɒf/
strange /streɪndʒ/
tax inspector /ˈtæks ɪnˌspektə(r)/
tax office /ˈtæks ˌɒfɪs/
the distance /ðə ˈdɪstəns/
trial /ˈtraɪəl/
witch /wɪtʃ/

UNIT 11 FAME AND FORTUNE

action /ˈækʃn/
award /əˈwɔːd/
bark (v.) /bɑːk/
bone /bəʊn/
box /bɒks/
cart /kɑːt/
champion /ˈtʃæmpɪən/
charity /ˈtʃærətɪ/
chocolates /ˈtʃɒkləts/
closing date /ˈkləʊzɪŋ deɪt/
competition /ˌkɒmpəˈtɪʃn/
complete (v.) /kəmˈpliːt/
contestant /kənˈtestənt/
criteria /kraɪˈtɪərɪə/
cruise (n.) /kruːz/
cucumber /ˈkjuːkʌmbə(r)/
demo tape /ˈdeməʊ teɪp/
deserve /dɪˈzɜːv/
editor /ˈedɪtə(r)/
empty-handed /ˌemptɪ ˈhændɪd/
fall /fɔːl/
finalist /ˈfaɪnəlɪst/
foolish /ˈfuːlɪʃ/
general knowledge /ˌdʒenrəl ˈnɒlɪdʒ/
get dark /get ˈdɑːk/
get sth sorted out /ˈget ... ˌsɔːtɪd ˈaʊt/
greeting /ˈɡriːtɪŋ/
handicapped /ˈhændɪkæpt/
hard luck /ˌhɑːd ˈlʌk/
homeless /ˈhəʊmləs/
host /həʊst/
hostess /həʊˈstes/
in order to /ɪn ˈɔːdə tuː, tə/
in suspense /ɪn səˈspens/
jackpot /ˈdʒækpɒt/
judge (v.) /dʒʌdʒ/
justify /ˈdʒʌstɪfaɪ/
member /ˈmembə(r)/
mine (n.) /maɪn/
minibus /ˈmɪnɪbʌs/
nominate /ˈnɒmɪneɪt/
nomination /ˌnɒmɪˈneɪʃn/
nominee /ˌnɒmɪˈniː/
ordinary /ˈɔːdənrɪ/
part (n.) /pɑːt/
partner /ˈpɑːtnə(r)/
penny /ˈpenɪ/
place (at university) /pleɪs/
pride /praɪd/
prize /praɪz/
protect /prəˈtekt/
proverb /ˈprɒvɜːb/
provide /prəˈvaɪd/
quiz show /ˈkwɪz ʃəʊ/
raise money /reɪz ˈmʌnɪ/
reader /ˈriːdə(r)/
rescue /ˈreskjuː/
rider /ˈraɪdə(r)/
round (n.) /raʊnd/
runner-up /ˌrʌnər ˈʌp/
save (my, your etc) life /ˌseɪv ... ˈlaɪf/
signature /ˈsɪɡnətʃə(r)/
score (n., v.) /skɔː(r)/
unconscious /ʌnˈkɒnʃəs/
unusual /ʌnˈjuːʒʊəl/
winner /ˈwɪnə(r)/
wise /waɪz/

UNIT 12 REVISION

advertising agency /ˈædvəˌtaɪzɪŋ ˌeɪdʒənsɪ/
bandit /ˈbændɪt/
businessman /ˈbɪznɪsmən/
celebrate /ˈselɪbreɪt/
cholera /ˈkɒlərə/
coincidence /kəʊˈɪnsɪdəns/
crash /kræʃ/
document /ˈdɒkjʊmənt/
downhill /ˌdaʊnˈhɪl/
dreaming spires /ˌdriːmɪŋ ˈspaɪəz/
epidemic /ˌepɪˈdemɪk/
feel /fiːl/
flight /flaɪt/
hesitate /ˈhezɪteɪt/
in (my, your etc) mind /ɪn ... ˈmaɪnd/
Israel /ˈɪzreɪl/
reunion /riːˈjuːnɪən/
shadow /ˈʃædəʊ/
typical /ˈtɪpɪkl/
visa /ˈviːzə/

Irregular Verbs

Infinitive	Past tense	Past participle
be /bi:/	was /wɒz, wəz/ were /wɜ:(r), wə(r)/	been /bi:n/
become /bɪ'kʌm/	became /bɪ'keɪm/	become /bɪ'kʌm/
blow /bləʊ/	blew /blu:/	blown /'bləʊn/
break /breɪk/	broke /brəʊk/	broken /'brəʊkn/
bring /brɪŋ/	brought /brɔ:t/	brought /brɔ:t/
build /bɪld/	built /bɪlt/	built /bɪlt/
burn /bɜ:n/	burnt /bɜ:nt/	burnt /bɜ:nt/
buy /baɪ/	bought /bɔ:t/	bought /bɔ:t/
catch /kætʃ/	caught /kɔ:t/	caught /kɔ:t/
choose /tʃu:z/	chose /tʃəʊz/	chosen /'tʃəʊzn/
come /kʌm/	came /keɪm/	come /kʌm/
cost /kɒst/	cost /kɒst/	cost /kɒst/
do /du:/	did /dɪd/	done /dʌn/
drive /draɪv/	drove /drəʊv/	driven /'drɪvn/
eat /i:t/	ate /eɪt/, /et/	eaten /'i:tn/
fall /fɔ:l/	fell /fel/	fallen /'fɔ:ln/
feed /fi:d/	fed /fed/	fed /fed/
fight /faɪt/	fought /fɔ:t/	fought /fɔ:t/
find /faɪnd/	found /faʊnd/	found /faʊnd/
fly /flaɪ/	flew /flu:/	flown /fləʊn/
forget /fə'get/	forgot /fə'gɒt/	forgotten /fə'gɒtn/
freeze /fri:z/	froze /frəʊz/	frozen /'frəʊzn/
get /get/	got /gɒt/	got /gɒt/
give /gɪv/	gave /geɪv/	given /'gɪvn/
go /gəʊ/	went /went/	gone /gɒn/
grow /grəʊ/	grew /gru:/	grown /grəʊn/
have /hæv/	had /hæd/	had /hæd/
hear /hɪə(r)/	heard /hɜ:d/	heard /hɜ:d/
hide /haɪd/	hid /hɪd/	hidden /'hɪdn/
hit /hɪt/	hit /hɪt/	hit /hɪt/
hold /həʊld/	held /held/	held /held/
hurt /hɜ:t/	hurt /hɜ:t/	hurt /hɜ:t/
know /nəʊ/	knew /nju:/	known /nəʊn/
leave /li:v/	left /left/	left /left/
let /let/	let /let/	let /let/
lose /lu:z/	lost /lɒst/	lost /lɒst/
make /meɪk/	made /meɪd/	made /meɪd/
mean /mi:n/	meant /ment/	meant /ment/
meet /mi:t/	met /met/	met /met/
pay /peɪ/	paid /peɪd/	paid /peɪd/
put /pʊt/	put /pʊt/	put /pʊt/
read /ri:d/	read /red/	read /red/
ride /raɪd/	rode /rəʊd/	ridden /'rɪdn/
ring /rɪŋ/	rang /ræŋ/	rung /rʌŋ/
run /rʌn/	ran /ræn/	run /rʌn/
say /seɪ/	said /sed/	said /sed/
see /si:/	saw /sɔ:/	seen /si:n/
sell /sel/	sold /səʊld/	sold /səʊld/
send /send/	sent /sent/	sent /sent/
set /set/	set /set/	set /set/
shine /ʃaɪn/	shone /ʃɒn/	shone /ʃɒn/
sing /sɪŋ/	sang /sæŋ/	sung /sʌŋ/
sink /sɪŋk/	sank /sæŋk/	sunk /sʌŋk/
speak /spi:k/	spoke /spəʊk/	spoken /'spəʊkən/
stand /stænd/	stood /stʊd/	stood /stʊd/
steal /sti:l/	stole /stəʊl/	stolen /'stəʊln/
swear /sweə(r)/	swore /swɔ:(r)/	sworn /swɔ:n/
take /teɪk/	took /tʊk/	taken /'teɪkn/
teach /ti:tʃ/	taught /tɔ:t/	taught /tɔ:t/
tell /tel/	told /təʊld/	told /təʊld/
think /θɪŋk/	thought /θɔ:t/	thought /θɔ:t/
throw /θrəʊ/	threw /θru:/	thrown /θrəʊn/
wake up /weɪk 'ʌp/	woke up /wəʊk 'ʌp/	woken up /ˌwəʊkn 'ʌp/
wear /weə(r)/	wore /wɔ:(r)/	worn /wɔ:n/
win /wɪn/	won /wʌn/	won /wʌn/
write /raɪt/	wrote /rəʊt/	written /'rɪtn/

Oxford University Press,
Great Clarendon Street, Oxford OX2 6DP

Oxford   New York
Athens   Auckland   Bangkok   Bogota   Bombay
Buenos Aires   Calcutta   Cape Town   Dar es Salaam
Delhi   Florence   Hong Kong   Istanbul   Karachi
Kuala Lumpur   Madras   Madrid   Melbourne
Mexico City   Nairobi   Paris   Singapore
Taipei   Tokyo   Toronto   Warsaw

and associated companies in
Berlin   Ibadan

OXFORD and OXFORD ENGLISH
are trade marks of Oxford University Press

ISBN 0 19 435767 8

© Oxford University Press 1998

First published 1998

No unauthorized photocopying
All rights reserved. No part of this publication may be reproduced, stored in a retrieval system, or transmitted, in any form or by any means, electronic, mechanical, photocopying, recording or otherwise, without the prior written permission of Oxford University Press.

This book is sold subject to the condition that it shall not, by way of trade or otherwise, be lent, resold, hired out, or otherwise circulated without the publisher's prior written consent in any form of binding or cover other than that in which it is published and without a similar condition including this condition being imposed on the subsequent purchaser.

Under no circumstances may any part of this book be photocopied for resale.

Printed in Spain

Acknowledgements
The author would like to thank all those at Oxford University Press who have contributed their skills and ideas to producing this book.

The author would like to thank his wife, Eunice, and his children, without whose support and patience *New Hotline* would not have been possible.

The author and publishers would also like to thank the ELT teachers and advisors who have given generously of their time to talk about their needs and to comment on *New Hotline*.

Illustrations by:
Ros Asquith, Clinton Banbury, Nicki Cooney, Belinda Evans, Hannah Firmin, Michael Hill, Sarah Jowsey, Christina Maloney, Colin Mier, Mark Oldroyd, Judy Stevens, Duncan Storr, Rob Taylor, Raymond Turvey, Lis Watkins.

The publishers would like to thank the following for their permission to reproduce photographs:
Allsport, The Bridgeman Art Library, British Museum, Collections (Liba Taylor), Chris Fairclough Colour Library, Sally and Richard Greenhill, Robert Harding Picture Library, Image Bank, Kobal Collection, Mander and Micheson, Network (Robert Hutchings), Paramount (courtesy Sipa, courtesy Kobal), Mark Pepper, Popperfoto, Rex Features (Blackburn, Dave Hogan), Science Photo Library, Sipa, Sygma (S. Cardinale, Dusko Despotovic, C. Kirkland), A Tannenbaum, John Walmsley, Warner Brothers (courtesy Kobal), Zefa Pictures. The picture of the monk on page 82 is of St Dominic by Carlo Crivelli (c. 1435/4 0 – c.95) Museo Stibbert, Florence/Bridgeman Art Library.

Victoria Road Photography by John Walmsley.

Location photography by Emily Anderson, Gareth Boden, Al Cane.

Studio photography by Mark Mason, Stephen Oliver.

The characters in Victoria Road were played by:
Safia Barakzai, Kay Dudeney, Michelle Harding, James Harvey, James Jones, Jessica Lam, Damien Matthews, Anna Mishcon, Sapana Mody, Mike McGee, Sylvester Odozi, Robert Page, Paul, Pat and Sarah Rose, Aurelia Riccio, Richard Sheehan, Patrick Short, Beccie Smith, Debbie Tidd, Lisa Walmsley.

The publishers and author would like to thank the following for their help with the Victoria Road story:
Ashtead Hospital (Surrey), Bootleg Musical Instruments (Epsom), Julian Bowman, BP Petroleum (Malden Rushett), Epsom College, Epsom Methodist Church, Epsom and Ewell High School (West Ewell), First Sport (Kensington) Guildford School of Acting, Health Education Authority, The Music Company (Crawley), NESCOTT Drama Department, Saville and Holdsworth (Surbiton) St Andrew's School (Leatherhead), Surrey County Youth Theatre, Therfield School (Leatherhead), Thorndike Youth Theatre (Leatherhead), Tiley's Hair Salon (Epsom), Rose and Brian Walsh, Wilson's Car Saleas (Epsom).

The publisher and author would like to thank the following organizations for their help and cooperation:
Base Cuts (Portobello Road, London), Channel 4 News, The Lovespoon Gallery (Swansea), Nick Morbath.

The publisher and author would like to thank the following for their kind permission to use articles, extracts or adaptations from copyright material. There are instances where we have been unable to trace or contact the copyright holder before our printing deadline. If notified, the publisher will rectify any omissions at the earliest opportunity.
'Hair'–poster from a Robert Stigwood production.
'Do wah diddy' used by kind permission of Carlin Music Ltd (Iron Bridge House, Chalk Farm, London).
'Born to be Wild' used by kind permission of Manitou Music Ltd (Canada). All rights administered and controlled by MCA Music.
'Oh Boy' (West/Tilghman/Petty) used by permission of MPL Comms. Inc., USA Peermusic (UK) Ltd., London.